SECRETS

SECRETS

THE FINAL BOOK IN THE SEVEN TRILOGY
FRED ELLIS BROCK

Wyatt-MacKenzie Publishing
DEADWOOD, OREGON

SECRETS
Fred Ellis Brock

The Third Novel in THE SEVEN Trilogy

ISBN: 978-1-948018-93-7 Trade Paperback
Library of Congress Control Number: 2020949620

The characters and events in this book are fictitious. Any similarity to real
persons, living or dead, is coincidental and not intended by the author.

Wyatt-MacKenzie Publishing
DEADWOOD, OREGON

Wyatt-MacKenzie Publishing, Inc., Deadwood, OR
www.wyattmackenzie.com

The Near Future

CHAPTER 1

Through the rain and fog, Bill Sanders could barely make out the White House from the window of his room at the Hay-Adams Hotel. He and Jake McCoy were having a late-night Scotch. They were in a pensive mood.

Jake looked up from his drink.

"Have you heard anything from Max?"

"No, but he returns to D.C. tomorrow. He didn't fly back with the President. He stayed in Cleveland for a follow-up story on Jim Winston. It's not every day that a President's press secretary commits suicide. What the hell should we do now?"

"Well, first thing we need to do in the morning is for me to call Jim Waters in Tucson and for you to call your lawyer in New York and tell them to cancel our 'button-down' arrangement. I think we should tell them to keep the envelopes we gave them in case we want to reactivate the plan. Then I guess we should meet with Max and talk about what to do next. After that, maybe I should return to Tucson and you go back to New York for a while. Let things simmer. I think I've gotten all I'm going to get out of my CIA friends. Not that they're holding anything back. They're as baffled by what's going on, or not going on, as we are. Coupled with your Pentagon source dumping you and warning you to drop The Seven, I'd say we've hit a plateau, or a ditch."

Bill nodded and sipped his Scotch.

There was a long period of silence, followed by a question from Jake.

"What time will Max get back tomorrow?"

"I'm not exactly sure. Sometime early in the afternoon.

He said he'd call me as soon as he got into town."

"Maybe the three of us can have dinner tomorrow night, and then you and I can head out the next morning."

"Good plan. I need to get back to work. My agent and publisher have been very patient, but there's a lot of money riding on this next book. However, I've made it clear—and they understand—that I may have to pull away from my writing from time to time over the next month or two. They know nothing about The Seven, of course. Only that I'm committed to finding out what happened to the ten-year-old daughter of my friend who died, they think, as the result of an auto accident in Indiana last year."

Jake drained his glass and sat it on the coffee table.

"I'm ready for bed. We'll talk tomorrow. Don't forget to call that lawyer in the morning."

"I won't."

Jake pulled his cell phone out and called a car service to take him to the Mayflower Hotel, where he was staying.

"Normally I'd walk. But not on a night like this."

Jake then put his hand on Bill's shoulder.

"Don't worry. This will all work out. It has to."

"I hope you're right."

"I usually am."

Jake picked up his jacket and headed for the door.

Once Jake was out of the room and headed for the elevator, Bill poured himself another, smaller drink of Scotch.

This is insane. I'm neck deep in a conspiracy that could pull me under at any moment. I should be in New York working on a book about the Middle East, not in D.C. worrying about how to stop a coup against the U.S. government. How could a single phone call from an old friend get me so involved in such a mess?

Bill finished his drink, picked up the hotel phone, and requested a 7 a.m. wakeup call. He then got undressed and crawled into bed. In less than five minutes he was sound asleep.

Bill was looking at the White House but not from his hotel room. He was standing in Lafayette Square. The West Wing was to his right.

It had quit raining, but the sky was full of dark, ominous clouds.

The White House was on fire! Flames were licking at the windows of the upstairs living quarters. Uniformed Secret Service agents were standing around talking to each other, apparently oblivious to the burning White House.

Bill started to run across Pennsylvania Avenue to warn the agents, but he stumbled and fell.

When he got up, he was no longer in Lafayette Square. He was standing in the clearing in front of Paul Watson's house in Indiana. It was night, and the sky was clear and full of stars that were brighter than usual. They were moving about, forming strange patterns. All the lights in the house were on. The front door was open.

Cindy Watson was standing in the door. She was wearing green pajamas. Paul had said she was wearing green pajamas the night she was abducted.

"Cindy?"

"Mr. Sanders?"

"Cindy, what are you doing here? You're dead?"

"I know, but I'm scared. I can't find my mom and dad."

The girl began to cry.

As Bill started walking toward her, she vanished.

Puzzled, Bill went inside the house. There was a gently burning fire in the fireplace. Sitting on the same sofa where Bill had discovered Paul passed out last year, were the late Colonel Richard West and Bill's wife, Jane, who was killed in a plane bombing more than three years ago.

Bill started to shout.

"What the hell is going on? Where did Cindy go?"

Suddenly, Paul Watson came out of the kitchen into the living room.

"No need to shout, Bill. We're all dead, but we can hear you. Why are you here?"

"I'm not. I mean, I was in front of the White House moments ago and now I'm here. I'm confused."

"Who isn't?"

Jane stood up, smiled at Bill and started walking toward the front door, which was still open. Colonel West joined her, and they walked out the door into the clearing. Bill started after them, but Paul grabbed him by the arm and pulled him back.

"Let them go."

Bill looked through the doorway into the dark yard, but Colonel West and Jane were gone. They had disappeared into the night.

Bill turned back to Paul, but he was also gone.

"Hello, Bill."

The voice that Bill knew so well was coming from the downstairs guest bedroom, just off the living room. He stepped into the room to find Morgen Remley sitting on the edge of the bed. She was dressed exactly the same as when he first met her at the library in New York last year: blue jeans, sneakers, and a yellow T-shirt. Her blond hair was tied in a ponytail.

"Bill, we have to talk."

"I know."

Suddenly, there was a blinding flash of light followed by a loud explosion. The house went dark.

He reached out for Morgen ....

Bill jerked awake as another rumble of thunder echoed in the distance and a flash of lightning lit up his room. He was clutching a pillow and covered in perspiration. He looked at his watch: three-fifteen.

Bill lay back on the bed and tried to relax. The thunder and lightning outside were oddly soothing. He had always liked thunderstorms.

The dream remained clear in his mind.

For two years after Jane was killed, Bill had a reoccurring nightmare in which he tried and always failed to keep her from boarding the ill-fated flight from Paris to New York. But for the last year or so, because of his involvement with Morgen, he believed, Jane's role in his dreams had shifted. He no longer was trying to save her. She was strangely distant, sometimes barely acknowledging him. She sometimes appeared with Colonel West, a man she never knew, and Bill had met only once. Morgen often was in the dreams with Jane.

Morgen. The woman he loved. The woman who he had thought betrayed him. But maybe not, according to Colonel

West's letter.

Bill rolled over and tried to go back to sleep. The thunderstorm was moving away.

Then next thing he knew his bedside phone was ringing.

"Hello."

"Good morning, Mr. Sanders. This is your wakeup call. It's seven and the skies have cleared. The temperature is sixty-eight degrees."

"Can you connect me to room service?"

"Of course. Hold on, please."

After a couple of clicks of the phone, Bill was connected. He ordered coffee, orange juice, and a full breakfast of bacon and scrambled eggs.

It was almost nine by the time he had eaten breakfast, shaved, showered, and dressed. He spent twenty minutes looking through The Washington Post. Max Burris's byline was on two stories with a Cleveland dateline, one about the services for Jim Winston. The other was an account of the President's activities in Cleveland, including a visit with Winston's parents and sister.

A little before nine-thirty, Bill called Bob Bowers in New York.

"Hey, Bill. What's up. It's not Friday yet."

"I know, Bob. I'm calling to tell you to cancel that agreement we made. But please keep that envelope in your safe just in case I need to reactivate our arrangement. I'll explain all this to you later. I promise."

"Okay, but don't forget the will."

"I won't. I'll be back in New York in a couple of days. I'll give you a call, and we can get together and take care of it."

"Good enough. See you then."

"Thanks. Bye."

Next Bill called Jake's cell.

There was no answer; the call went to voice mail. Bill hung up without leaving a message.

A few minutes later his cell phone chimed. It was Jake.

"I was afraid you'd disappeared."

"Not a chance. I was in the shower."

"So, what are your plans for the day?"

"I'm assuming we'll get together with Max for dinner tonight. You said he'd call you when he gets back in D.C. this afternoon, right?"

"Yes."

"Then I'm going to spend at least part of the day visiting an old aunt of mine I haven't seen in years. She lives on Dupont Circle. She'll soon be ninety-four and is as sharp as a tack. Or was last year when I talked to her on the phone. She knows everybody. She was friends with Alice Roosevelt Longworth, who lived nearby. Maybe I should ask her about The Seven. Just kidding. What are you going to do?"

"There's a couple of rare bookstores I used to like when I was living here and working for the Times. Assuming they're still in business, I thought I'd check them out."

"Sounds good. Give me a call when you hear from Max."

"Will do. Bye."

"Later."

Bill decided to walk to the bookstores. It was a pleasant morning, and the fresh air put him in a good mood. That good mood soured a bit as he walked past the White House and noticed two armed snipers on the roof. *This town has turned into an armed camp. Sad, but necessary, I guess. What the hell will happen to it if The Seven makes a move? What will the military do? Or is it infiltrated by The Seven? Larry Sullivan said The Seven was top-secret and was being 'handled' by the military. What does that mean? That the military is pushing back against The Seven? Or helping them?*

Bill was having a late lunch at a sushi bar. He was feeling better. He had splurged at one of the bookstores and bought a signed, first edition copy of *As I Lay Dying,* by William Faulkner. He smiled as he tried to imagine Faulkner in a sushi bar.

It was almost two when his cell phone chimed. It was Max.

"Hey, Max. Where are you?"

"At Reagan National. I need to stop by the office for an hour or so, but then I'll be free. Any plans?"

"Jake thinks the three of us should have dinner tonight and discuss things. He's flying back to Tucson tomorrow, and I'm returning to New York."

"Sounds good. But instead of going to a restaurant, why don't we eat at my place. I can order some food to be delivered. It'll be much more private. Say seven-thirty?"

"Sure, but where do you live?"

"At the Watergate."

"The Watergate?"

"Yep. In fact, my apartment is on the same floor as Monica Lewinsky's old apartment. I inherited some money a couple of years ago and decided that was a good place to invest it. Plus, I get a nice place to live."

"I guess. If the ghosts don't bother you."

"Not a bit. I don't believe in them anyway."

"Jake and I will be there at seven-thirty then?"

"Perfect. Is Thai food okay?"

"Sure."

"When you get here, just check with any of the doormen. They'll call me and then direct you to my apartment."

"Will do."

Bill called Jake, who thought meeting at Max's apartment was a good idea. He was amused that Max lived at the Watergate.

"Brings back memories. I was around during the Watergate scandal. Hunt and McCord. The Saturday night massacre. Dangerous times and dangerous people. Way out of control. But that's ancient history now. And a reminder that I'll soon be seventy-three years old."

"I saw *All the President's Men*. Good movie. How about if I get a car and driver and pick you up at the Mayflower at seven?"

"I'll be waiting in the lobby, smart ass."

Bill walked back to the Hay-Adams. Once in his room, he took a quick shower and changed clothes. He tucked the Faulkner book into a side pocket of his suitcase. He looked at his watch and was surprised to see that it was only five-fifteen. He pulled *As I Lay Dying* back out of his suitcase, settled into a club chair, and began to read. *The curse of being an English major.*

At six, he pulled himself away from the world of Addie, Jewel, and Cash and ordered a car and driver for six-forty-five. He continued to read until he had to head to the front of the hotel and his car.

✳

Max's apartment, decorated in Danish modern, afforded a spectacular view of the Potomac River. Bill, Jake, and Max had drinks on the balcony while they waited for the food to be delivered.

"I took the liberty of ordering for all of us. Spring rolls. Pad Thai with shrimp. Red curry with chicken and coconut milk. Medium hot. Hope that's okay."

Bill and Jake nodded their approval.

So far, they had not spoken of the reason for their meeting. Bill decided it was time.

"Were there services for Leon Jenkins?"

Jake looked puzzled.

"He's the editor who was killed by a hit-and-run driver in front of the Post."

"Oh, right."

Max poured another round.

"No services. He had been divorced for years and his ex-wife died two years ago. He was cremated and his ashes will be flown to Nebraska, where his only brother lives. He was a loner and apparently had left instructions with a lawyer that there were to be no services or memorials. There was nobody to even clean out his desk. One of the clerks put everything in a box and sent it to the lawyer. You know I've been in Cleveland covering Jim Winston's funeral for the past few days. I just heard the details about Jenkins when I stopped by the office this afternoon. What the hell did he do to piss off The Seven?"

"Maybe he just got really nervous and panicked when he saw his name on one of the lists we mailed," Jake replied. "Maybe The Seven thought he would do something rash. Maybe he tried to quit. That's apparently not an organization you can just walk away from, as West pointed out in his letter to Bill."

The apartment phone buzzed.

Max stood up.

"It's our food."

It was after eight and the three were hungry. They talked little as they ate the spicy food and washed it down with bottles of cold St. Paulie Girl beer Max had pulled out of his refrigerator.

After dinner, they settled in the living room and resumed their conversation.

Jake spoke first.

"Look, here's what I think is going on. I believe The Seven is in a panic mode right now. They don't know who sent the lists, the summaries, and pictures. I don't think they suspect Bill is involved. Or me. But one wrinkle is the reaction of Bill's Pentagon source in warning him away. If he's aligned with The Seven, your inquiry could be a red flag. But if he's not, then nobody knows. We're still invisible. I tend to think the latter is true. Otherwise, they would have moved against us by now. If they're as rattled as I think they might be, and if Bill's Pentagon source isn't involved with them, then that gives us a lot of space."

Bill interrupted.

"But if my Pentagon source isn't involved, why did he change his phone number?" *Jake is the only one here who doesn't know Larry Sullivan's name. Max does because he helped me reconnect with him last year.*

"That's pretty standard. If he ran up against some really heavy stuff, he might not want to talk to you for some time."

Max brought some more cold beers from the kitchen.

"So, what do we do? I've got to go back to work at the Post tomorrow and pretend I don't know the truth about Jim Winston. When I was in Cleveland it was really weird talking to the President and realizing he didn't know that one of his closest aides was involved in a plot to overthrow him. At least, I assume he doesn't know."

"That's what Colonel West wrote in the letter he had sent to me after his death."

Jake lifted his beer mug to take a drink, but then he sat the mug back down on the coffee table and looked at the other two men.

"It's getting late. I'm flying to Tucson tomorrow, and Bill's heading back to New York. Let's call it a night. But let's stay in touch and let things stew for a while. Right now, The Seven seem to be in a holding pattern. My CIA and NSA contacts will let me know if they think something is happening. Let's use this time to figure out how to build our forces, as Colonel West advised, from the outside toward the center.

CHAPTER 2

Bill settled into a first-class seat on the Acela a few minutes before the high-speed train was scheduled to depart. He had picked up copies of The New York Times and The Washington post at a newsstand in Union Station. He glanced at the front pages, folded the papers, and tucked them into his backpack.

As the train rolled north toward New York and home, Bill ordered some coffee. Cream, no sugar. He was in an odd mood. He wanted to get back to work on his Mideast book, which he had tentatively titled *Power Points*. But he was tortured by events of the past year or so that had interrupted his somewhat monastic life and put him on a collision course with a powerful, secretive group called The Seven that he had learned was responsible for his wife's death and the deaths of two hundred other people on her plane. And the death of his best friend and the kidnapping and murder of his friend's ten-year-old daughter. Plus, a young reporter who was getting too close to the truth. Was that only the beginning? Was the murder of the United States next? And what about the dark secret behind it all: the coverup of the reality of UFOs and aliens from God-knows-where. Or to be more precise: the coverup of what the government doesn't know about UFOs and aliens.

Bill took a deep breath and a sip of coffee. The Acela was on the outskirts of D.C., heading into Maryland. He reached into his backpack and pulled out a notebook and a mechanical pencil.

I know I wrote a summary for the "button-down" package Jake wanted. But that was for others to read. It was only a summary; I left out a lot of personal elements, including feelings and emotions. I need to start at the beginning and put together a chronology of events that have carried me to this point. An accounting for me. Maybe compiling it will help me understand things better.

He opened his notebook and began to write.

First things first. It was three Decembers ago that Jane, my soul-mate and wife of 26 years, was killed when a Paris to New York flight she was on was blown up over Newfoundland. A suicide bomber connected to a Middle East jihadist group was blamed at the time. It was only recently that I learned the truth.

I had left a newspaper career and The New York Times eight years earlier to write books. It was tough at first. I published a couple of true-crime books, a genre I decided wasn't for me. Jane and I spent the next two years traveling around Mexico and Central and South America, researching Points South, *my breakthrough book, which is part travel and part politics. Nancy Luke, my agent who had encouraged me at every step, got an advance for the book that was bigger than I had ever dreamed. I spent another year writing it. The hardback version was on The New York Times best-seller list for almost a year. The hardback royalties and paperback rights made more money than I had earned in twenty years as a reporter. Jane used to say it was that book that gave us our fuck-you fund: enough money so that we didn't have to do anything we didn't want to, ever again.*

Just after Jane was killed, I started writing a coming-of-age novel called Look Down. *It got rave reviews and hit the Times best-seller right off the bat. It's still there. Nancy sold the film rights to English-Frostmann Studios for a million dollars. Jack Turner, "Mr. Hollywood" himself, will direct the movie. It's being filmed in Jefferson, Indiana, later this summer. I was back in Jefferson in March to help Turner scout sites for filming. I promised I would try to return when the filming starts in August.*

Right now, I'm working on a book about the Middle East called Power Points. *It's modeled after* Points South, *a combination of travel and politics.*

It was right after I'd finished Look Down *and was struggling with the structure of* Powers Points *that Paul Watson called. I had just returned from a month-long trip to rural Vietnam and Cambodia where*

I was researching a chapter I wrote for an anthology a friend was editing.

An attendant interrupted Bill's writing.

"Would you like some lunch, Sir? We have some excellent sandwiches."

He handed Bill a menu.

Bill studied it briefly.

"I'll have a tuna salad sandwich on whole wheat and some more coffee. Also, a bottle of water."

"Very good, sir."

"By the way, where are we?"

"We'll be coming into Baltimore in about fifteen minutes."

"Thanks."

Bill returned to his notebook.

That call from Paul started my trip down the rabbit hole. But I had no choice. I couldn't say no to him, not after he begged for my help. He wouldn't tell me what was wrong but wanted me to come to our hometown of Jefferson, where he worked as a guidance counselor at the local high school. He said he had no one else to turn to. He said he would explain when I got there.

Thinking and writing about Paul's call for help forced the past into the present, whether Bill wanted it or not.

Bill and Paul had become friends in the fifth grade, just after Bill's family moved to a farm they bought near Jefferson. They were Kentucky tenant farmers who had finally saved enough money for a down payment on forty acres of land across the Ohio River in Southern Indiana. Bill's brother, Ron, was born later that year. By then Bill and Paul Watson had become fast friends—more like brothers, really. Bill and Ron were never close. Years later Ron was killed in a prison fight in Texas, where he was serving a life sentence for killing a deputy sheriff in a drunken brawl. Bill's parents had died seven years earlier, only six months apart. The three deaths left Bill with no immediate family, only some distant cousins in Kentucky he didn't really know. Until Paul's call for help last year, Bill had only returned to Jefferson three times since graduating from high school, twice for the funerals of his parents and once for his brother's funeral.

When I got to Jefferson last year, I learned that Paul's ten-year-old daughter, Cindy, had been missing for two weeks. The police thought she was a runaway, although at first, they suspected Paul and Sharon were somehow involved. But they were both cleared. Paul, who had started drinking heavily, told me he witnessed Cindy being abducted by a giant UFO. He said she was floating in a beam of blue light between her upstairs bedroom window and the alien craft. He also told his wife, Sharon, and the Madison County Sheriff, Dave Taylor, about the UFO. Sharon thought Paul was having a psychotic breakdown and left him; she went to live with her parents in Indianapolis. Dave, whom Paul and I went to high school with, also thought Paul was a mental case but kept the UFO story out of any official records. At the time I didn't believe Paul either. Only later, after he was dead ... killed ... did I learn he was telling the truth.

I didn't know it at the time, but Paul had a long history with UFO abductions. He didn't know about it himself until he started having "memory attacks" a year and a half before Cindy's disappearance. He wrote all this down in a notebook and was going to tell me about it. He never got the chance. I only know because I discovered his notebook when I was in Jefferson recently with Jack Turner, the Hollywood director.

Bill stopped writing and finished his sandwich. He ordered another cup of coffee. The train was somewhere between Baltimore and Philadelphia. Bill put his notebook away and upfolded the newspapers from his backpack. But he couldn't focus on them. He lay back in his seat and tried to relax, but he couldn't clear his mind.

Jane always said I was secretive and a loner. I used to counter that it would be more polite to describe me as modest and publicity shy. She liked to cut to the chase. But I was also a damn good reporter. I think it's because I'm so ordinary looking and acting. Regular height, regular features. Brown hair, brown eyes. Nothing threatening about me. I was a good interviewer because I knew when to shut up and listen. I also knew not to argue with my interview subjects. I wasn't the story. Now I am the story. I don't like it, but there's nothing I can do but see it through. Find a way out of the rabbit hole.

Bill was finally able to doze off. The next thing he knew the train was pulling into Penn Station in New York.

Bill took a taxi to Eastside Towers, his apartment building on East Seventy-Second Street. His apartment, 32-B, was on the thirty-second floor and had a commanding southern view of the East River and the United Nations building.

George Carson, the chief doorman at Eastside Towers, smiled as he opened the taxi door and helped Bill with his suitcase.

"Welcome home, Mr. Sanders."

"Thanks, George."

Once in his apartment, Bill unpacked his suitcase and looked around. He hadn't been gone that long but was glad to be back home among familiar surroundings. Jane had picked out the apartment and furnished it. It had a big living room and a galley kitchen next to a dining alcove. There were two bedrooms; one Bill used for an office. The décor was eclectic, but it seemed to work, thanks to Jane. A sofa, a club chair, and a wingback chair were arranged in the center of the living room.

Bill looked at the club chair, remembering that was where Morgen usually sat when they met at the apartment. The musky smell of her perfume had lingered in the chair for weeks.

Bill walked over to the south-facing window and looked out. It was a clear day; he could see the Statue of Liberty.

Why the hell don't the goddamn aliens just land in front of the U.N. building or on the south lawn of the White House and announce their presence? That would put an end to The Seven and their murders and plots.

Paul shuddered as he suddenly remembered something he had read when he was researching UFOs and alien abductions with the help of Morgen. An anthropologist was speculating on the existence of aliens and, if they were real, why they didn't make contact with us. His answer: "These beings could be thousands or millions of years ahead of us in technology and evolutionary development. Would you expect an entomologist studying an ant colony in the Amazon to try to make contact with the ants? To be overly concerned if he accidently stepped on one and killed it?"

Colonel West said the aliens seemed indifferent to us unless they felt threatened. Can the nation and the world live with the knowledge that we are being observed or studied, and abducted, by creatures who won't communicate with us? The government obviously thinks not. That's why The Seven was created by President Truman. To create the public perception that the government knows what is going on and is keeping it a secret while, at the same time, ridiculing anyone who takes UFOs and aliens seriously. The only time I met West was in some secret bunker that was an hour and a half drive from New York. He put it this way: "Think about it and consider the government's position. Can you imagine what would happen if we were to confirm that UFO sightings and aliens are real? What if we said to the public: Yes, these craft and beings from we-don't-know-where routinely invade our air space, kidnap our citizens, mutilate our cattle—and we know nothing about the who or the why of any of this. We are powerless, absolutely powerless, to do anything. We don't know whether they are here for good or for evil reasons. And, oh, by the way, we suspect they can read our minds and might be altering our genetic makeup. Can you imagine what would happen to the fabric of society? To religions? To government institutions? To government authority? To the stock market?"

But in the letter Colonel West had arranged to be delivered to me more than six months after he died, he had changed his mind. He was convinced The Seven had become too powerful and was far more dangerous than the results of the public knowing the truth about UFOs and aliens. He believed The Seven was planning a coup against the government. He wanted me to stop it. Me! An ill-equipped soldier in a shadow war. But it was the only way I might get Morgen back. Plus, West had played his ace in the hole: He told me The Seven killed Jane. That she was collateral damage, along with the other passengers on the plane. The target: a congressman who was planning public hearings to investigate The Seven.

Bill walked over to a bookcase in his office and pulled down a copy of *The Rise and Fall of the Third Reich*, by William

Shirer. Tucked inside was the original copy of Colonel West's letter from the grave.

Bill's home phone rang.

He closed the book around the letter and put both back on the shelf.

"Hello."

"Bill, it's Nancy. You answered your home phone, so you must be back in New York."

"I got in just a few minutes ago. What's up?"

"Can we have lunch tomorrow? I know it's out of our regular schedule, but I really need to talk to you.

"Sure. What time?"

"Is twelve-thirty good for you? I'll make reservations."

"Perfect. See you then."

There was no need to mention where. Bill and Nancy Luke had been having monthly lunches at Dave's for years. The restaurant was a bit overrated, but Nancy liked it because it wasn't popular with agents and the literary crowd with their endless gossip. It was also midway between her office near Rockefeller Center and Bill's apartment on the Upper East Side.

Bill knew he owed no small part of his success as a writer to Nancy, one of the top literary agents in New York. She had believed in him and stood by him when he was struggling after leaving The New York Times to write books. He was her top-earning client, but he hadn't always been. And despite their professional relationship, which was based on a bedrock of success and money, they weren't close friends. Nancy came from a monied family. She had grown up in New York, Martha's Vineyard, and Europe. She was married to a wealthy international lawyer. Bill grew up dirt poor in Kentucky and Indiana. Nancy was guarded and self-protective. Some people described her as detached. That fit well with Bill's penchant for secrecy. He and Nancy seldom discussed anything personal. At book parties she and his publisher arranged, he often wondered if he was the only one there whose family had ever had a car repossessed. His motivations to succeed were clear.

Nancy's were subtler, based on family standards and a sense
of duty.

＊

The next day also was clear and sunny. Bill decided to
walk to Dave's.

He arrived at the restaurant at twelve-fifteen. Gerald,
their usual waiter, greeted him with a wave. There was no
sign of Nancy. Gerald escorted him to their usual table.

"Would you like something to drink now or would you
prefer to wait for Ms. Luke?"

"I'll wait for Nancy. But I would like a bottle of water."

"Right away."

Nancy showed up a few minutes later. She looked terrific
as always. Her body looked younger than her face, which was
wrinkled from too much sun. She loved the Caribbean; she
and her husband flew there three or four times a year. They
had just returned from Barbados in March when Bill and
Nancy had met for lunch just before he flew to Jefferson to
meet Jack Turner. Nancy was pushing fifty, but she could easily
be confused for a woman in her late thirties. Bill remembered
thinking in March that her hair looked lighter than usual.
Now it seemed even lighter. Bill mentally scolded himself and
stopped thinking about how Nancy looked or what she did
with her hair. He reminded himself how important she was
to his financial success as a writer. In addition to big advances
on books, there was that million dollars she got for the film
rights to *Look Down*. Thanks to Nancy, he had enough money
so that he never had to worry about it again. She got fifteen
percent off the top and was worth every penny.

Bill stood up and gave Nancy a kiss on the cheek. She
squeezed his hand.

Once she was seated, Gerald took their drink orders and
gave them menus. Each had a glass of Santa Margherita Pinot
Grigio.

"So, what did you need to see me about?"

"Jefferson and Jack Turner."

"What about them?"

"Jack called last night. He said you were tentative about whether or not you would come to Jefferson when they start filming, depending on how your writing was going. You were certainly tentative when you talked to me about it. You said you 'hoped' to go. Then you asked me if I wanted to go with you."

"Do you?"

"Yes. But first things first. Jack wants you to absolutely commit to being in Jefferson for a week during the filming. The reason is that his nephew, who is a documentary film maker who won an Academy Award a couple of years ago, wants to make a documentary on the making of the movie version of *Look Down*. A film about a film, I guess. Needless to say, he wants you in it. They've agreed to a fat consulting fee even bigger than what you got for helping Jack scout Jefferson in March. Of course, they'll pay all expenses. Plus, they'll fly you to Jefferson and back in the English-Frostmann jet, the same as they did earlier. You can't say no to Jack on this, Bill."

"You'll go with me?"

"I said yes."

"Okay. I'll go. Do we know the exact date?"

"Not yet, but I should know in a few days."

Gerald interrupted to take their orders.

"The special today is penne pasta with lobster and a mild lemon-butter sauce. I recommend it."

Nancy shook her head.

"I'll have the broiled salmon with rice instead of potatoes."

"Very well. Sir?"

"I'll try the penne and lobster."

"Excellent. Will that be all?"

Both nodded.

When Gerald disappeared into the kitchen, Nancy smiled.

"I stopped ordering pasta out. The last time I did, I dripped red sauce all over a white suit I was wearing. Too messy. But I love it."

CHAPTER 3

President Samuel Stanton was sad and irritated at the same time.

Sad because he had recently returned from Cleveland and funeral services for Jim Winston, his press secretary who had committed suicide. Jim, a former Ohio newspaperman, had been with him since he was elected governor of Ohio and from there decided to make a run for the White House. He was with him when he was re-elected President for a second term. Beyond being his press secretary, Jim was also his friend. They understood and trusted each other. Nobody in the administration could speak for the President with the authority of Jim Winston. The President knew he had to replace him, but doubted that he would ever be able to share the same confidence and trust with someone else. Like everyone who knew Jim, the President was confounded that he took his own life. Why? There wasn't a hint that anything was wrong. He apparently didn't leave a suicide note.

The President was irritated because a public housing bill he wanted passed was stuck in a Senate subcommittee. He had just gotten off the phone with Ross Duncan, the majority leader, who was dragging his feet on the bill. Duncan clearly wanted some kind of quid pro quo, but never said exactly what it was. He promised to get back to the President tomorrow morning. The President was puzzled. The usually decisive and direct Duncan seemed distracted and unfocused, even a little confused. He acted like something more important was on his mind.

Drumming his fingers on the Resolute Desk, the President picked up his phone.

"Yes, Sir?"

"Martha, I have a two o'clock meeting with Cole Favate, right?"

"Yes, Mr. President."

"I'm free until then?"

"You're supposed to call Senator Benton."

"That can wait. He just wants to pressure me not to close that Army base in Iowa. I'm going to go up to the residence in a few minutes for some lunch. I'll be back by one-thirty. One other thing, Martha. When I meet with Colonel Favate, I don't want to be interrupted for any reason short of a nuclear attack. The meeting is scheduled for an hour, right?"

"Yes, Sir."

"Well, it shouldn't be any longer than that. Remember, no interruptions."

"I'll remember, Sir. Don't worry. Should I alert the staff that you're coming to the residence?"

"No. I'm just going to make a turkey sandwich for myself. I don't need a production."

"Very good, Mr. President."

After his lunch of a turkey sandwich and a glass of almond milk, the President spent a few minutes channel-surfing among cable news programs. The big news seemed to be a story with visuals of a dog being rescued from a well somewhere in Vermont. *Must be a slow news day. Good.*

Shortly after one-thirty, he returned to the Oval Office. He was accompanied by two Secret Service agents. He again reminded Martha, who had been his secretary since he was elected more than six years ago, that he didn't want to be disturbed during his meeting with Colonel Favate.

The President turned to the two Secret Service agents.

"Same for you guys. I do not want to be disturbed during this meeting for any reason. Is that clear?"

"Yes, Sir," both said in unison.

"We'll be just outside the door as usual," one added.

Martha and the two agents left, closing a curved door behind them.

The President—a big man with sharp features and black hair mixed with streaks of gray—settled into the leather chair behind his desk. He looked across the room at the portrait of Thomas Jefferson hanging to the left of the fireplace. Behind the painting was a hidden safe. Thinking about what was inside always caused his chest to tighten.

He reached under the edge of his desk. There were two buttons. The one on the right would summon the Secret Service. The President then pressed the button on the left. It was linked to the White House surveillance center and shut down the hidden video cameras and audio recorders that recorded activity in the Oval Office. He had fought with the Secret Service for two weeks after he was first elected for the ability to make the office "dark" when he wanted privacy.

His phone buzzed.

"Yes?"

"Sir, Colonel Favate's car has just pulled into the compound. He'll be here in a few minutes."

"Good. Show him right in."

"Yes, Sir."

The president looked again at the portrait of Jefferson. The photographs in the safe behind it were proof that he had been lied to by top people in his administration, especially at NASA. He had also become suspicious of Robert Walker, the CIA Director. Walker was a longtime friend of the President; they had been roommates in college. Yet the last few times they had talked, the President was sure Walker had been lying to him. He could tell by his voice. He just wasn't sure about what. Or why.

He knew he wasn't supposed to have these pictures. They were dangerous. Cole Favate, his childhood friend from Ohio and now an Air Force colonel assigned to the Defense Intelligence Agency at the Pentagon, had given them to him a little more than a year ago.

It was after a state dinner at the White House for the Italian prime minister. Cole and his wife, Karen, were at the dinner. Afterward, Cole asked the President if they could have a few words in private. The President led the way into the Oval Office, where he switched off the hidden video cameras and recorders.

Without saying a word, Cole pulled the three envelopes from inside his dress tunic and handed them to the President.

Only then did Cole speak. "I'm giving you these envelopes because you're my friend," he said. "They're self-explanatory. I can't say anything more about them except that I'm not supposed to have them, and you're not supposed to see them. My career—hell, my life—would be in danger if anyone knew. After you look at the contents, destroy them."

"Cole ..." the President began.

"Please, Mr. President," Cole interrupted. "Don't ask me anything. Just trust me and do as I say. We must never discuss this again."

Then Cole abruptly left, leaving the President dumbfounded and alone in the Oval Office with the three numbered envelopes.

The President immediately locked them in his safe and walked back to the State Dining Room to say his farewells to the departing guests.

The President did not destroy the pictures. Since the night Cole gave them to him, he took the pictures out of the safe every two weeks or so and studied them, usually with a magnifying class he kept in his desk drawer. They showed beyond a doubt that NASA and the military, and maybe other agencies, had been lying to him and the American people about the famous "face" on Mars and about the existence of UFOs. He never discussed the pictures with anyone, including Cole. That was about to change.

A knock on the door told him Cole was here.

"Come in."

The curved door opened, and Martha escorted Cole into

the Oval Office. She nodded to the President, turned, and left, quietly closing the door behind her.

The two men shook hands warmly, obviously glad to see each other. Cole was wearing his full-dress uniform.

"Let's sit over here," the President said, pointing to facing blue- and gold-striped sofas in front of the fireplace.

"You want some coffee or anything, Cole?"

"No thanks, Mr. President. I just had lunch."

"How's Karen?"

"She's good. She sends her regards. We just had our twentieth anniversary, as you know. Thanks again for the Chinese vase."

The President nodded.

In an awkward moment following the mention of an anniversary, the President glanced across the room at a gold-framed picture of his wife on a corner of the desk. She died the summer after he was re-elected to a second term. They kept her cancer a secret during the campaign, always hoping she would beat the odds and recover. He briefly considered resigning when she died, but he knew that was only an expression of self-pity.

"Sir, I was sorry to hear about Jim Winston. I didn't know him as well as you, but whenever I dealt with him, he was always fair and honest."

"I know. It's not the same around here without him. I've got to find a new press secretary, but no one can replace Jim."

"Does anybody know why he would take his own life."

"Not a clue."

Cole started to say something, but the President held up his hand.

"Cole, you're my best friend. We've known each other since we were children. We grew up together. We trust each other fully. Right?"

"Absolutely."

"I called you here because we have to talk about something that you warned me a year ago never to talk about. It's those pictures you gave me. I still have them. I didn't destroy them like you told me to do."

"Mr. President, how private is our conversation right now?"

"You mean is it being recorded?"

"Yes."

"It is not. Not in any way. I've personally turned off all audio and video recorders. This office is dark. What's said between us is between us. Let's agree not even to make notes afterward. There will be no evidence this conversation ever took place."

"Can we be frank?"

"Of course. Forget I'm the President. Let's talk like we used to back in Ohio. Just don't call me Sammy. I always hated that nickname."

"I know you did. Don't worry, Mr. President ... Samuel."

"Look, Cole, I've worried and fretted over those pictures since you gave them to me. I couldn't destroy them like you asked me. When you gave them to me you said your life could be in danger if anyone knew you had them. Why did you say that?"

"Because those pictures are classified above top secret. They're not available to you or any President. Maybe I was exaggerating a bit, but both the guy who gave me the photos and I would be in some deep shit if it were discovered we had them. I wanted you to destroy them to break the link to me."

"Well, I didn't. They're just too important. Do you understand what they mean?"

"I guess they mean E.T. is here. And that face on Mars, which NASA has always said was simply the result of a play of light and shadows, is actually some kind of man-made ... alien-made? ... structure."

"That's exactly right. The face is enormous. A mile wide. Carved from the stone of the Martian surface. And the sides of those triangular-shaped objects, which I assume are alien craft, are a quarter of a mile long. Who gave you those pictures?"

"A friend at NASA. I think he gave them to me because he

knows you and I are friends. I think he wanted the President to see them."

"Well, the President has seen them, and he's pissed off. The existence of those pictures means that I've been lied to and misled by people I trusted. The reality, the secret, that those pictures represent could be explosive if made public in the wrong way."

"I don't understand something, Sir. There have been UFO sightings and stories of aliens and abductions for decades. There have been sightings by the military recorded on radar. It's not as if the subject is a secret."

"I know. I know. There seem to be two contradictory scenarios going on at once. One is that the government knows a lot about UFOs and aliens, which it keeps a lid of secrecy on. There are even stories that the government has agreements that allow the aliens to study us, and abduct us and mutilate our cattle, in exchange for advanced technology. But if that were the case, don't you think the President would be in on it? I guarantee you he isn't. The other scenario is that there is no such thing as UFOs or aliens, and anybody that studies them or takes them seriously is a kook. That's why most serious scientists won't touch the subject. They would be subject to ridicule. They'd be cut off from grant money. Do those contradictory lines stem from the same source? If so, why? Have any Presidents known about the reality behind these photos? Remember, poor Jimmy Carter became a laughingstock when he reported seeing a UFO."

"Didn't this all start with Truman and Roswell?"

"I guess. But the Pentagon has said over and over again that there was nothing to Roswell."

"True, Sir. But the Pentagon did release those Navy radar sightings of UFOs from a few years ago. It also owned up to spending twenty-two million dollars to investigate the UFO phenomena at the urging of Harry Reid, who was Senate majority leader at the time."

"Let's think about this from another angle. Tell me something, Cole. Have you noticed anything a little strange or weird lately? I mean like a feeling or a sixth sense that something is about to happen or that something's not right."

"Yes, for sure. Things got really odd about a month ago. The sense that something big was about to happen was palpable. Scuttlebutt was that the Chinese were going to do something big. Invade Taiwan, maybe. But little was spoken. It was like a feeling that permeated the ranks of the people I work with."

"There was nothing about this in my briefings."

"Maybe that's because it was too amorphous. Also, I'm not sure whatever this feeling was ever rose to a high enough level to involve the Joint Chiefs or the Oval Office. But here's the really weird thing. About a week ago, it all stopped. Everything went quiet. No rumors. No gossip. No scuttlebutt. No nothing. People didn't want to talk about it. It was as if the apprehension of an impending event had never existed. If somebody like me brought it up, many people would change the subject, or look away, or walk away. It was the strangest thing."

"Is it still that way?"

"More so. It's as though a lot of people are afraid of something."

"Cole, do you think what you've been describing could have anything to do with those pictures you gave me?"

"I never thought about it, but off the top of my head I don't see any connection. Why?"

"Nothing. Just a thought."

The President got up and walked over to his desk. On it was a silver tray containing a carafe of ice water and two crystal glasses. The President filled both classes with water and carried them across the room. He handed one to Cole.

"Cole, I need someone I can trust who's not political and not Cabinet-level. I need you. I want you to be my eyes and ears in the real world outside of this bubble in which I am forced to work and live. I never know whether people are telling me the truth or just kissing my ass because they want something or just because I'm the President. Will you speak truth to power, even if the truth you speak may not be what power wants to hear?"

"To you, Sir, always. You know that. We've known each other too long."

"Yes, I guess we have. Okay, here's the deal. I think something is going on, and I think it's being kept from me. I don't know what, why, or by whom. But something big is up. I brought this up in a phone call with Walker at CIA. He suggested I needed more rest. I could tell by his voice that he was lying to me. Hell, we were roommates in college. I know when he's lying. But I don't know why or about what. Maybe it has to do with those pictures. They prove NASA, and presumably the Pentagon, has been lying. They prove the existence of UFOs and aliens from God-knows-where. But why the secrecy? I can understand why that might be kept from the public, although I'm not sure that's a good idea in the long run. But from the President of the United States? There's got to be more to this than just keeping UFOs a secret. Something else is going on. I should discuss this with my Chief of Staff, but we don't go back a long way, and I'm just not comfortable bringing something this vague—and let's face it, weird—up with him. He's pretty buttoned-down, if you know what I mean. That's a hell of a position for a President to be in. We've got to get to the bottom of this, Cole."

"I'll do my best to help, Mr. President."

"I know you will. Let's plan on meeting once a week from now on. If you need to talk to me between meetings, call Martha. She'll get you in here. I don't think we should discuss anything over the phone. At least not at this point."

"I agree."

"One other thing, Cole. Do you know Max Burris, the Post reporter?"

"Slightly. I've meet him at a few cocktail parties. Why?"

"He doesn't know it yet, but he's on a short list of candidates for press secretary to replace Jim. I don't know him that well. He flew out to Cleveland with me on Air Force One, and we got to talk some. He seems like a good guy."

"That's my impression. His reporting is right down the middle. He seems fair-minded. A straight shooter."

"Well, we'll see. The Burris thing is confidential. Let's talk in a week and see where we are."

After Cole had left, the president sat, lost in thought, at his desk. The Oval Office was still "dark." He started to push the button to restore the recordings when there was a knock at the door.

"Come in."

Martha opened the door and came into the office. She had been crying and was holding a white envelope in her hand.

"What is it, Martha? What's wrong?"

"Mr. President, we were cleaning out Jim Winston's desk. I was just overcome with sadness. And we found this. It's for you."

She handed the white envelope to the President. It was a standard White House envelope. The flap was taped down. On the front in Jim Winston's handwriting were the capitalized words: THE PRESIDENT. EYES ONLY.

Martha sniffed, turned, and left the Oval office for her own desk just outside the door.

The president peeled the tape from the envelope. Inside was a folded piece of standard-issue White House stationery. In the center were five lines of writing, all in capital letters:

THE SEVEN
ROSS DUNCAN
ROBERT WALKER
THREE SS
SNAKEBITE

Chapter 4

Bill Sanders was having a bowl of soup for lunch at his dining room table and looking out the south-facing window of his apartment. Lower Manhattan had been fogged in all morning, but the haze was beginning to clear.

Bill had gotten up early and had been working for several hours on *Power Points*, his book about the Middle East. He needed a break.

He finished his soup and walked into his office. He rummaged around in his backpack and found the notebook in which he had started writing a personal record of the events of the past year or so, mainly focusing on a trip to his hometown of Jefferson, Indiana, after a friend there begged for his help. He began writing a chronology of these events in the notebook on the train returning from Washington last week. He always thought more logically when he wrote. He hoped a written rehash of events might help him understand things better. Or see things more clearly. Or make connections he had missed.

Bill skimmed what he had written on the train. He picked up a pencil, walked into the living room, and sat in the club chair. He began to write.

Although skeptical of Paul's story that Cindy was abducted by a UFO, I agreed to help him find his daughter, or find out what happened to her. Two things softened my skepticism. The first was that Paul told me a couple of things he had told no one else. When he saw Cindy floating in the beam of blue light, she was being returned to her room, not taken from it. He also said he heard the sound of a helicopter. This was right before he became unconscious in the clearing in front of their isolated house. Sharon was in their bedroom, also unconscious and unaware of what he said was happening. At the time Paul told me this, it didn't make sense. If Cindy was being returned to her room, where had she been? The second thing that gave me pause was that I found out the next day that there had been a number of UFO sightings around Jefferson during the past year. All the descriptions were of large triangular craft just like Paul said he saw above his house. I remember his words clearly: "A big goddamn machine shaped like a triangle, bigger than the house and the clearing, was just hanging there in the sky about a hundred feet over the roof ... it was absolutely silent."

Bill was interrupted by the ringing of his office phone. He answered it by the fourth ring.

"Hello."

"Bill?"

"Yes."

"Bill, it's Neal in Jefferson. I hope I'm not interrupting you."

"Not at all. What's up?"

"I'm trying to track down some rumors on the movie for the Courier. You're my best source. Is it true that Jack Turner moved the start date for filming to mid-August? It must be, since English-Forstmann has reserved every room in town starting then."

"That's what I understand. Why don't you call Turner?"

"I tried, but he's out of the country. And I couldn't reach his assistant, Joan Wilson. She's apparently with him."

"Well, based on what my agent said—and those hotel bookings—I think you're safe to go with that."

Neal had another question.

"Also, I heard a rumor that Turner's nephew, who's a documentary film maker, is making a film about the making of *Look Down*. Also heard that the documentary will feature a lot of you. Is that true?"

"Yes, according to my agent. But I don't know much more than that. I don't even know the name of Turner's nephew."

"It's Richard. Richard Turner."

"Tell me something, Neal. How do you pick up on all these stories way out there in Indiana?"

"I'm just a natural-born news hound. I talk to people. I also listen. Like you. Or like you were before you moved to books. Say, this documentary means you'll be coming out here for sure when they start filming, right? You were less than certain about coming when we had dinner at my house with Turner and Wilson."

"I'll be there. My agent, Nancy Luke, is coming with me."

"Do you know exactly when you're arriving?"

"Not yet. But I'll let you know. Sometime in August, I assume."

"Well, if you can't find a hotel room, you and Ms. Luke are welcome to stay with Marge and me. We've got three guest rooms in that big house."

"Thanks. I may take you up on that offer."

"Sure thing. So long, now."

"Bye, Neal."

Bill walked back to the living room and again settled into the club chair. He picked up his notebook and pencil, but instead of writing he started thinking about the phone call he had just received.

Neal—his name was Graham Neal, but he had never been called anything but Neal—was the editor of the Jefferson Courier. He had hired Bill to cover basketball games while he was in high school and later hired him as a reporter during the summers between his college years. Neal's family had owned the newspaper for almost a hundred years. He taught the young Bill Sanders a lot about reporting and even more about human nature and how to deal with people. Bill knew that Neal and Nancy Luke were two people to whom he owned a great deal. When Bill had gone to Jefferson last year to help Paul, Neal was one of the first people he contacted. Neal was in his mid-seventies but showed no signs of slowing down or retiring. When Bill was in Jefferson in March to help Jack Turner scout spots to film *Look Down*, Neal and Marge had hosted a dinner at their house for Bill; Turner; Joan Wilson, Turner's assistant; and John King, the Courier reporter who was covering the movie story.

Bill turned his attention back to his notebook.

After hearing Paul's story, I talked to Dave Taylor, the Sheriff who had investigated Cindy's disappearance. He thought Paul needed psychiatric help and that his UFO "experience" was a hallucination or a lie. Dave, like Neal, had little patience for UFO stories and thought the recent sightings in Jefferson were the results of overactive imaginations fueled by alcohol or drugs, or both. Neal had downplayed news coverage of the sightings, even though some UFO investigators had come to town. Dave and I agreed to share anything we found out with each other, a promise I soon broke. I tried to talk with Daniel Scott, the Courier reporter who had been covering Cindy's disappearance and the UFO sightings, but he wasn't at the paper when I stopped by. I left word I would see him the next day.

Then things started to happen fast.

First, Paul's house was broken into and ransacked when he and I were at a restaurant having dinner. Nothing seemed to have been taken, although my cell, an old-fashioned flip phone I had left in the guest bedroom, was smashed. Only later did I learn that destroying that phone was an effort by The Seven to force me to get a smart phone so I could be traced more easily. And there was a threatening note in my duffel warning me to leave Jefferson. The house phone lines were also cut, apparently to remove a listening device that had been installed earlier. We drove into town around midnight to report the break-in, only to discover that Daniel Scott had committed suicide by shooting himself in the heart.

The next day, I managed to slip into Daniel Scott's room at a residence hotel where he lived. There I found a map of Jefferson and surrounding Madison County on which Daniel had placed a series and Xs and Os. At the bottom of the map, he had written "O = UFO sightings" and "X = helicopters." I took the map. I never told Dave Taylor about it, breaking my promise to share information with him. It wasn't the first time. I also hadn't told him about the threatening note that was left in my duffel.

I convinced Dave Taylor to run a paraffin test on Scott. It proved that he did not fire the gun. He was murdered. So now the map I found in Daniel's room meant I was withholding evidence in a murder investigation.

The next day, Paul, who was now drinking heavily, crashed his Jeep into a concrete culvert on a rural road. He died shortly afterward at the hospital. His last word to me was "... 'copter." Later I talked to a farmer who witnessed the crash. He said there was a strange-looking black helicopter flying low over the road just before the crash. Dave Taylor dismissed the story because of the farmer's notoriously bad eyesight.

Bill's cell phone chimed. It was Max Burris.

"Hey, Max. What's up?"

"Don't sound so goddamn cheerful. We need to talk. But not on the phone. I'm about two blocks away from your apartment. Eastside Towers, right? I had to come to New York for an interview at the U.N. Tonight's your night to finally buy me that dinner. If you're free, that is."

"Absolutely. The doorman's name is George. I'll tell him to expect you. I'm on the thirty-second floor. Apartment 32-B."

"Okay. See you in a few minutes."

Bill alerted George and then picked up his dish and glass from the dining room table and put them in the dishwasher. He glanced around. The apartment looked pretty good. His cleaning lady had been there two days ago.

He sat back down in the club chair. He put his notebook and pencil into the drawer of a table next to the chair.

As he was waiting for Max, his mind began to drift. He thought of Morgen, wondering where she was. If Colonel West was right, she should try to get in contact with him if she could. West said she had soured on The Seven. He sent her the same kind of letter from the grave that he sent Bill. Bill thought of their nights in Brussels and Bruges when they had traveled together to Belgium last year in search of the then mysterious Colonel Richard West. He remembered the first time they made love. Their twenty-year age difference melted away that rainy day in the Brussels Hilton. He knew then that he loved her. He still loved her, no matter what she had done.

Bill's reverie was interrupted by a knock on his door.

He and Max shook hands as Max came into the apartment.

"Christ, you teased me for living at the Watergate. This ain't exactly a tenement. My God, look at that million-dollar view!"

"Jane picked this place. Furnished it, too."

"She had great taste ... sorry to use past tense. You know what I mean."

"Yes, I do. It's all right. It's been more than three years now. I'm coming to terms with her death. Although learning that she was killed by The Seven has been tough to deal with."

"I know. But we need to talk. First, can I have a glass of water?"

"Do you want something else. A drink? Some food?"

"Nope. Just water."

Bill went into the kitchen and came back with two glasses and two bottles of Evian water. Bill offered Max the wingback chair that was sitting at a forty-five-degree angle to the club chair he settled into.

Max took a long drink of water.

"Have you talked to Jake?"

"Not since we left D.C. I need to call him. What did you want to talk about? If it's this mess with The Seven, I don't know any more than I did in D.C. Do you?"

"No, but I have some interesting news. It looks like I'm on a short list of people being considered by President Stanton to replace Jim Winston as his press secretary. I may know by tomorrow or the day after."

"Congratulations. How did you find out?"

"When the FBI came calling. I was scared shitless at first that their visit had something to do with The Seven."

"Will you take the job if Stanton offers it?"

"Oh, hell yes. I couldn't turn that down. I could always go back to the Post or to any other number of good jobs. Plus, I could get used to riding on Air Force One."

"Do you know Stanton all that well?"

"Not really. We've talked a few times, most recently in Cleveland. He strikes me an honest guy. After all, he's in his second term and nobody in his administration has been indicted."

"You realize if you take that job it'll get a member of our little group of three inside the White House. Knowing what you know, would you use that position to help block whatever the hell The Seven's up to?"

"Of course. That's the first thing that crossed my mind when the FBI showed up."

"We need to talk, but let's get dinner settled first. What are you in the mood to eat tonight? We can always get a great steak at Smith and Wollensky. There's also a good Italian restaurant I like and a French bistro, both within walking distance. Or do you have someplace in mind? Your choice?"

"Let's go to Smith and Wollensky. I'm in the mood for steak."

"Is seven-thirty okay with you?"

"Sure. That'll give us plenty of time to talk."

"When are you going back to D.C.?"

"Tomorrow afternoon. I've got an interview at the U.N. at ten in the morning."

"You're welcome to stay here. The sofa's pretty comfortable."

"Thanks, but I've already checked in at the Hilton on Sixth. Left my suitcase there."

Bill got up and walked over to the computer in his office. He found the phone number for Smith and Wollensky and made their dinner reservation.

Bill returned to the club chair.

"Max, do we know anything more about Jim Winston's suicide? Was it really suicide?"

"I guess so. From what you've told me wrist-slitting is not one of the methods favored by The Seven. They seem to prefer guns and stolen cars. Besides, I checked the police report on Jim. He was locked inside his apartment, and there was nothing to indicate anyone else had been there. The neighbors heard nothing."

"Do you think he killed himself because his name was on the lists that Jake and I mailed? Was he scared or feeling guilty?"

"Hard to say. I thought I knew him pretty well. We worked together for several years at The Plain Dealer in Cleveland. The Jim Winston I knew would never have gotten involved with The Seven. Maybe he was being blackmailed, but I can't image for what. Maybe it was guilt. Maybe he suspected or knew what The Seven was planning. Maybe he felt trapped. If he tried to spill the beans, The Seven would kill him. If he said nothing, he would become part of a treasonous coup. I would like to think that when he first became part of The Seven, he did so because, like West and your girlfriend ... what's her name?"

"Morgen. Morgen Remley."

"I'd like to think he did so because, like West and Morgen Remley, he initially believed that keeping the government's ignorance of UFOs a secret was important to national security. But as time went by and he became more and more aware of The Seven's accumulation of power and what it had morphed into, he became disillusioned. Maybe he wanted out but realized there was no way. Maybe when he saw what happened to Leon Jenkins, whose name was also on the list, he freaked. Maybe. Maybe. Maybe. Hell, I just don't know."

"Well, if you wind up at the White House, we need to get Jake back here so the three of us can make some serious plans. I don't want to talk to him on the phone about anything. You taught me that lesson last year. Maybe we should all try to meet in D.C. tomorrow or the day after."

"Tomorrow. The sooner the better. If Stanton names me his press secretary, I assume he would give me at least a few hours' notice. But once he does it, I'm going to be really busy for the first few days."

"No doubt. Let's text Jake and see if we can meet tomorrow."

Bill picked up his cell phone and punched in a text: "Can we meet tomorrow in D.C.?"

Within less than a minute the phone pinged that there was a reply: "Yes. Will call early afternoon."

Bill put the phone down.

"Well, that's that. I'll be at the Hay-Adams if I can get reservations. I'm sure Jake will stay at the Mayflower. Hold on a minute."

Bill got up, walked into his office and logged on to this computer. He booked a room at the Hay-Adams. He also reserved a seat on the Acela.

"Okay. I'm set at the Hay-Adams. Maybe the three of us can have dinner tomorrow night."

"Let's plan on it. My best guess is Stanton won't make an announcement until the next day. Of course, if he picks someone else, no problem."

"I'm betting on you, Max."

"Thanks. We'll know soon enough."

"Max, I want to talk to you about Larry Sullivan. Other than Morgen, you're the only person who knows that he was a valuable source of mine at the Pentagon for nearly a decade. He was the one who helped me in an effort to track down Colonel West last year after I came back from Indiana. When I talked to him last week, after seeking his help with The Seven, he completely rejected me. He said I was in over my head and that I shouldn't get involved. He said The Seven was top-secret and was 'being handled' by the military, whatever that means. He said secret plans and operations have been underway for months. He walked away. When I tried to call him later, I got a recording that said his number was no longer a working number."

"But didn't Jake say he doubted that Sullivan was involved with The Seven or they would have come after us by now?"

"Yes. He also said ditching a phone number was common in cases like this. But if Larry's not involved, he was clearly spooked by whatever he found. Spooked enough that he dumped our long relationship. I know he trusted me. He knew I would go to jail before I would reveal him as a source. The more I think about it, the more I think he was really scared of whatever he picked up. Maybe he was trying to protect himself. Maybe me. Maybe both of us. I wish I had a way to get in touch with him."

"You probably don't, but I'll bet the President's press secretary does."

＊

Bill and Max finished dinner a little after nine. It was raining lightly when they walked out of Smith and Wollensky on Third Avenue.

Max pulled out his cell phone and summoned an Uber for a ride to the Hilton.

"So, I'll see you and Jake tomorrow evening in D.C. You want an Uber? Do you have the app?"

"No. I'm a little behind the curve on technology. I'll get a regular taxi."

Max's Uber call pulled up to the curb. They shook hands and Max climbed into the car. Bill watched the red taillights recede into the mist.

Despite the rain, Bill hailed a taxi quickly.

The lobby of Eastside Towers was quiet. One of the night doormen, whose name Bill couldn't remember, was seated at a desk. He looked sleepy.

"Good evening, Mr. Sanders."

Embarrassed at his inability to remember the man's name, Bill waved and headed for the elevator bank.

Once in his apartment, Bill settled into the club chair. He had had two cups of coffee after dinner and was wide awake. He reached into the drawer of the table next to the chair and pulled out his notebook and pencil. He let his mind drift back to last year in Jefferson, Indiana.

After Paul's death, I called Warren Holden in Santa Fe. He was a former two-term senator who had helped me with Points South. *He had also once held hearings on UFO sightings and the military. He advised me to contact Walter Jansen at the Carter Center in Atlanta. Jansen had been a top aide to President Jimmy Carter, who claimed to have seen a UFO along with Jansen. I made arrangements to fly to Atlanta from Louisville the next day to meet him, but I missed my flight because of some mysterious truck fires on the I-65 bridge over the*

Ohio River, the route into Louisville and the airport. I rescheduled my appointment with Jansen and my flight for the following day. On the way back to Jefferson, I heard on the radio that Warren Holden had died from an apparent heart attack.

Convinced he had been murdered like Daniel Scott and afraid I might be next, I fled Jefferson and returned to New York. There I got a FedEx envelope from Warren that was sent the day before he died. It contained a piece of stationery with a single handwritten name: COL. (RET.) RICHARD WEST.

I was searching for Colonel West and reading about UFOs at the main branch of the library on Fifth Avenue when Morgen Remley introduced herself to me. She said she recognized me from my picture on the jacket of Points South, *which she said she admired and had obviously read carefully. She was a marine biologist looking for a full-time teaching job. She also said she was a part-time researcher for the Mutual UFO Network, or MUFON. A few days later I decided to trust Morgen. I was also attracted to her, despite our age difference. I called her and offered her a job as a research assistant to help me find West. I also told her all that had happened in Indiana. She accepted. She then gave me a crash course in the modern history of UFOs and alien abductions.*

We went to Washington to meet with Max Burris to see if he would help me reconnect with Larry Sullivan, an old Pentagon source of mine when I was with the Times. When I met with Larry, the years slipped away. He agreed to help me track down West, but it proved tough. He said West was protected by layers of secrecy. Prior to retiring ten years ago, West had worked for NATO for five years in Brussels. Larry gave me the name of someone who might have known him, so Morgen and I flew to Brussels. The Belgian contact, a retired American doctor, showed us a letter he had received nine years ago from West. It was postmarked Pine Bush, New York. We both recognized Pine Bush as a so-called UFO hot spot. It was also in Brussels and later in Bruges that Morgen and I became lovers.

Then things got really strange. I received a call from West. He wanted to meet with me and Morgen but only under unusual circumstances. We were picked up in front of my apartment by two, armed security men in a U.S. government SUV. We were blindfolded and driven for two hours. Then we were led into an underground bunker. Morgen and I were separated; I never saw or heard from her again.

I spent the rest of the night talking with Colonel West, who was obviously in pain and dying from cancer. That was when I learned of the existence and purpose of The Seven, and West confessed that the organization killed Cindy Watson; her father and my friend, Paul; and Daniel Scott, the Jefferson Courier's reporter. He said they were going to kill Warren Holden, but Warren saved them the trouble by dying of a heart attack. I also learned that Morgen was a Seven agent who had been used to lure me to West. West said he wanted me to come to work for The Seven. I rejected his offer and threatened to expose the murderous organization. West showed me a file and said if I did the file would be released to the press. It showed that I was an alcoholic drug user who had been hospitalized several times over the past decade for treatment of paranoid schizophrenia and delusions. I was blindfolded and returned to my apartment. My silence was the price of freedom. For almost a year, I was the only one outside of The Seven who knew the fates of Cindy Watson, Paul Watson, and Daniel Scott. Now Max and Jake know.

West died in August, within weeks of our meeting. A short obituary with few details ran in the Times.

Well into the new year, I received a letter from West, written just before he died. But he arranged to have it delivered six months after his death. In the letter West said:

· He had become disillusioned with The Seven but was in too deep and was too sick to take any action.

· He believed The Seven had become too powerful and was planning a coup against the U.S. government. The secret group may have assassinated John F. Kennedy because he was threatening to expose them.

· The Seven was responsible for blowing up the plane and killing Jane. The target was James Handforth, the chairman of the House Intelligence Committee, who was planning to hold public hearings to investigate The Seven.

· Morgen did not betray me in the end. She did what she did to save me. His exact words from his letter: "She loves you, but she realized you two could never be together as long as The Seven existed and you *wouldn't agree to work for them. She knew if she tried to quit, they would kill her. She did not betray you. She actually saved you by convincing me to blackmail you with the bogus file instead of killing you. I think she is as confused as the rest of us and has lost all faith in The Seven."*

Bill paused writing and looked at his watch. Eleven-thirty.

There was a quiet knock on his door. *Who the hell could that be? How did someone get past the doorman in the lobby? Maybe it was a neighbor. But at nearly midnight?"*

Before Bill had opened the door enough to see who it was, he knew. He could never forget that musky perfume.

"Hello, Bill," Morgen Remley said quietly. "We need to talk."

CHAPTER 5

The black SUV with opaque side windows bounced down a rutted gravel road leading to a log cabin nestled deep in the woods in the middle of a two-hundred-acre tract of land in Ulster County, New York, about fifteen miles north of the little town of Pine Bush in neighboring Orange County. The cabin and its front porch weren't visible from the macadam road that ran along the west side of the property. If a stranger drove down the gravel road, he or she wouldn't notice that every move was being tracked by hidden cameras and sophisticated electronic sensors buried in the ground and carefully camouflaged in trees and on fence posts. The cabin was part of an elaborate set to conceal what lay underground. It hid an elevator that descended to the entrance of a gigantic subterranean bunker with living quarters for twenty people. Branching off the bunker were connecting chambers crammed with electronic equipment, including two advanced Chinese Sunway supercomputers. It was one of two such secret installations in the United States. The other one, newer than the upstate New York facility, was in southern New Mexico, near the Mexican border.

The SUV stopped near the dimly-lighted front porch of the cabin. The driver and the front passenger were both wearing dark suits. When they got out of the SUV, the driver made no effort to conceal the Glock pistol under his jacket. The man who had been sitting in the front passenger seat opened the right rear door. An older man in casual clothes stepped out of the vehicle and walked to the front of it. He looked over the hood at the driver, silhouetted by the light from the porch.

"Is everyone here?"

"All except Mr. Walker, but you knew he wasn't coming."

Ross Duncan, the majority leader of the United States Senate, nodded and started walking toward the cabin. He climbed the four steps to the porch, opened the front door, and walked into a living room with an overstuffed sofa and chairs and a stone fireplace. He turned to the left toward an elevator and punched its single button. By now the driver and the other man were right behind him. The three entered the elevator. Senator Duncan punched another single button. The elevator doors hissed shut and it started to descend.

When the elevator stopped and the door opened, Duncan and the two men stepped out into a carpeted corridor and headed left toward a conference room. Duncan went into the room and closed the door behind him. The two men waited in the corridor by the door.

Duncan took a seat at the head of a large conference table. To his right was an empty chair where Walker usually sat. Two men in suits were also on the right, farther down the table. To Duncan's left was a man dressed in casual clothes. Farther down from him were two women, one in a business suit, the other casually dressed. All looked serious. None spoke or greeted Duncan as he sat down.

"I guess you all got the message that Robert Walker won't be here today. He had to go to a meeting at the White House. I'll fill him in later."

Duncan pulled a notebook from his back pocket and looked at some items he had scribbled on the first two pages.

"Before we get started, let's go over some things we discussed in New Mexico last month. First, Snakebite is still on hold, and Lockdown is still in effect. We've got some serious problems with those lists and summaries and pictures that were mailed all over D.C. from all over the West. We don't have any clue as to who the hell did that, or why. We assumed Holden had them, but despite two attempts we weren't able to find them at his house in Santa Fe. Thing got a little out of hand when our men killed that cleaning lady. I was afraid we were headed for an out-of-control situation like we had in Jefferson, Indiana, last year. Luckily, we were able to contain that. Then we find out from one of our people at the Carter Center that Walter Jansen had what we were looking for. He and Holden were close. Holden must have given them to him, maybe for safekeeping. We got them from his house, but because we feared he knew too much he had to be neutralized. We used our usual method with cars. But it was all wasted effort. Someone copied those lists and summaries and photos and mailed them to everyone on the lists. Are we still sure that Bill Sanders and the ex-CIA guy ...?"

"Jake McCoy," the man next to Robert Walker's empty chair volunteered.

"Yes, Jake McCoy. Are we still certain they weren't involved?'

"That's my area," the same man responded. "We're sure. Sanders visited Jansen in Atlanta, Holden's widow in Santa Fe, and McCoy in Tucson, but the visits were connected with research on his book about the Middle East. Both areas of expertise for Holden and McCoy. Sanders and McCoy couldn't have been involved in the mailings because they were in Tucson when the packets were mailed from dozens of post offices in as many states. We know this because we were able to track their cell phones. They never left Tucson. We're also rock solid sure that Sanders is too scared of that file we showed him to ever do anything. It would ruin him. He would never be able to prove it's fake."

A flash of irritation crossed Duncan's face.

"Well, crap. Somebody had to mail them. Our lockdown order for everyone to ignore them and keep quiet worked only so far. Leon Jenkins panicked and was about to go rogue on us. Earlier we had that blabbermouth drunk at the State Department. We had to do what we had to do with both of them. It was too bad about Jansen, but he posed a real danger to us. I think he had been talking to Holden and knew too much. Lucky for us, Holden had a heart attack. No such luck with Jansen. I'm afraid the Lockdown is fraying at the edges.

More people on those lists might panic. This could seriously threaten Snakebite, which is already on hold."

Duncan paused, but no one said anything.

Duncan continued.

"What about Jim Winston's suicide? What the hell was that about? Anybody have a clue?"

Five heads moved side to side in unison.

"He was an important source for us in the White House. He was close to Stanton. The three Secret Service agents are helpful, but they don't see the big picture. But if Winston was suicidal, he could have been a problem when we launch Snakebite. Maybe it's just as well."

No one said a word.

Duncan paused, poured some water into a glass from a condensation-covered carafe at his end of the table, and took a sip.

"One other thing. What about this colonel at the Pentagon who was asking around about The Seven? Who the hell is he? He's not one of ours."

One of the women to Duncan's left spoke up.

"We're not sure what he was up to, but our people put the fear of God into him. I don't think he's a problem anymore."

"What was his name?"

"Colonel Lawrence Sullivan."

"Wasn't he the same guy who was asking about Richard West last year?"

"Yes. He said some distant cousin of West was looking for him and thought Sullivan might be able to help. I don't think the West thing had anything to do with his recent questions about The Seven. Just coincidence."

"I don't like it. I don't believe in coincidences. Not this kind, anyway. Let me talk to Walker. I'll get back to you about Sullivan."

"Whatever you say."

CHAPTER 6

The sight of Morgen and the familiar smell of her perfume almost took Bill's breath away. He opened the door and she stepped into the apartment. She was pulling a small suitcase, which she propped against the wall inside the door.

"How did you get by the doorman?"

"He was sound asleep at his desk. I walked right past him to the elevators. I hoped you would be here."

Bill was nearly speechless. Morgen was as beautiful as he remembered. Her blond hair was hanging free around here shoulders. She was wearing a dark blue pants suit

He reached out to shake her hand. Morgen took his hand with both of hers and squeezed it. Then she wrapped both of her arms around his neck and pulled him tight against her.

She began to cry.

"I love you, Bill Sanders. I've wanted to contact you so many times but was afraid to try. Can you ever forgive me? Can we ever get back to where we were last year?"

Morgen's tears were soaking Bill's shirt. He could taste their salty wetness through strands of her hair stuck to his face and lips.

"Morgen, I've never stopped loving you. I forgave you a long time ago. I've just been waiting for this moment. We have a lot to talk about. I know about the letter you got from West. I got a similar one. He said you betrayed me to keep me safe and that you had quickly become disillusioned with The Seven."

"That's putting it mildly."

Bill wiped her tears from her face with his hand.

She stopped crying and smiled.

"Yes, we do have a lot to discuss. But tomorrow. First things first."

She took his hand and pulled him toward the bedroom.

✳

Bill and Morgen were up by eight. They were having coffee and toast at the dining room table and watching the morning sun glint off the U.N. building.

Morgen caressed Bill's arm.

"So, what do we do now? Where do we go from here? I told my Seven contact that I needed to come to New York to deal with some family legal matters, which is partly true. My father was born in the Bronx and still owns his family home there. It's rented, but he wants to sell it. He has heart trouble and shouldn't be traveling. I promised him I would meet with a real estate agent and get something going on selling the place. I've never seen the house. It may need some repairs.

"But something weird has been going on lately. Sometimes I got the feeling that The Seven people didn't really trust me. They seemed to follow my work a little too closely. But that all stopped a couple of weeks ago. They seemed to lose interest in me. They were upset and distracted. When I told them that I needed to leave Portland for a few days to come down here, they just shrugged and said to go ahead. I'm certain I wasn't followed or tracked. I left my cell phone back in Maine just to be on the safe side."

"You've been in Maine? Did you try to call me recently?"

"Yes, twice. But there was no answer. I didn't leave a message. I was using a friend's special burner phone that changes its number after you make two calls."

"That explains why, when I tried to call the number back, I got a recording say it was no longer a working number. I assumed it was a robo-call."

"It was me."

Morgen took a sip of coffee.

"Back to my original question. What do we do now?"

"As you said last night, we need to talk. But I have to go to D.C. for two or three days. I have a reservation this morning on the 11:35 Acela. I have to go. It has to do with The Seven and Max Burris. Remember him, the reporter from the Post who helped me get in touch with my old Pentagon source?"

"Of course."

"I'm also meeting someone else I've been working with. An ex-CIA agent named Jake McCoy."

Morgen gave Bill a blank look.

"A lot has gone on since our hooded ride last year. Some of it you may know. Much of it I'm sure you don't. I assume you know a lot I don't. I have an idea. Why don't you come with me on the train to D.C. That'll give us at least two and a half hours to talk and fill each other in. Then you can turn around and take the train back here. I'll come back as soon as I can, maybe tomorrow. The next day at the latest. You shouldn't be seen in D.C., especially with me."

"I guess that would work. That would give me time to take care of my business here."

"I'll give you a key and let George know you'll be staying here."

"I already have a key, remember? You gave it to me last year. Our parting didn't exactly lend itself to returning the key."

"You're right. I had forgotten all about it."

Bill got up, walked into his office, logged onto his computer, and bought a round-trip train ticket for Morgen. He then called the desk phone in the lobby.

"George, it's Bill Sanders. Remember Morgen Remley, the blond woman who was working for me for a time last year?"

"Yes, of course."

"Well, she's back for a while. I'll be out of town for two or three days, and she'll be staying in my apartment. She has a key. Please give her whatever assistance she needs."

"Of course, Mr. Sanders."

"One more thing, George. Could you arrange a car to take us to Penn Station at ten-thirty?"

"Consider it done."

"Thanks, George."

✳

The first-class car of the Acela was not crowded. Nevertheless, Bill and Morgen talked quietly.

"Let's start at the beginning. Or the end. Where were we taken last year after we were hooded and driven by those two guys for a couple of hours?"

"Upstate. Ulster County, a few miles north of Pine Bush. The Seven has a secret facility there. They have another in New Mexico, on a big ranch. I've only been there once. In a helicopter from Las Cruces."

"Pine Bush! I suspected that. It's where the letter was from that West sent to that doctor friend of his we talked to in Brussels. Plus, it's a UFO hot spot. It was one of the cases you gave me to study. And New Mexico. Another UFO hot spot. That probably explains the fishing trip."

"Fishing trip?"

"I'll tell you later."

"I'm not sure how much any UFO activity around Pine Bush had to do with The Seven putting that facility near there. Remember what West told you: The aliens pretty much ignore us, and we don't have a clue what they're up to. I just think The Seven was looking for a remote place not too far from New York City. For New Mexico, just remote."

"What happened to you after we stepped out of the elevator and were separated?"

"I was taken to Stewart Air National Guard Base in Newburgh, where I was put on a government jet and flown to Rome. I was there for almost two months before I was reassigned to Maine. I've been there ever since working to discredit a couple of academics who were getting too close to the truth about The Seven."

"Are you succeeding?"

"I'm ashamed to say I am. But I had no choice. You know

that by now. Because of me—and The Seven's success at making anyone who takes UFOs seriously look like a kook—these two professors have had their grant money pulled and their research project canceled."

"How long had you been working for The Seven when you introduced yourself to me at the library?"

"About a year. My assignment was to sort of reel you into Colonel West and The Seven. They wanted you pulled in carefully. They really hoped you might agree to work for them. But I really was a fan of you and *Points South*."

"What about your roommate from Kansas I met on our way to JFK when we flew to Brussels?"

"An actress. Hired for the day and paid very well. As am I."

"And you didn't grow up with an uncle in Kansas after your parents were killed in a car crash?"

"Nope. Born and raised in L.A. I was an only child. My parents still live there. But I really do have a doctorate in marine biology."

"I know. I checked that out after the first time we met. I should have dug a little deeper."

"The Seven had already done that. I was prepared for anything you might have found or asked. The only thing The Seven, and I, didn't count on was us falling in love."

Bill smiled and squeezed Morgen's hand.

An attendant brought lunch menus. They both ordered club sandwiches and bottled water.

"So, you were aware of that bogus file that West threatened me with if I went public."

"I helped create it. I convinced them that it would make you clam up. Otherwise, if you didn't go to work for them, they were prepared to kill you. Although at that point, West was so soured on The Seven I'm not sure he would have let it happen. That is, if he could stop it. I think the death of your friend Paul's ten-year-old daughter, along with West's terminal cancer, prompted him to write those letters to us. He had mellowed. He was not as cold and hard-ass as he pretended when he talked to you."

Morgen took a bite of her sandwich and looked directly at Bill before continuing.

"Make no mistake. West was right. The Seven has become extremely powerful and is operating way beyond its original charter. Its leaders are planning a coup against the United States government. They call it Operation Snakebite, which I know only from a conversation I overheard. But something happened recently to cause them to put it on hold. I wasn't close enough to anyone in Maine to get the lowdown. But there was talk that some members had been exposed through some lists that had been mailed to a lot of people in D.C. It wasn't clear to me. Have you heard anything about that?"

"Morgen, Jake McCoy and I sent those lists. Along with summaries explaining them and some NASA photos that prove the existence of UFOs and aliens."

"Whoa. Back up. Tell me everything that happened from the time you left the New York bunker and West."

Bill spent the next hour filling Morgen in on the past year: his winter trip to the Middle East for research on *Power Points*; his early spring trip back to Jefferson to help Jack Turner scout scenes for the movie version of *Look Down*; his discovery of Paul's notebook with the description of Paul's "memory attacks" of being abducted by aliens as a boy; his second trip to the Mideast in the late spring; the letter from West that caused him to seek out Walter Jansen and Betty Holden, Warren Holden's widow; Jansen telling him to seek out Jake McCoy, Jansen's longtime friend and an ex-CIA agent with an interest in UFOs; the break-in, theft of a file cabinet, and the murder of a cleaning lady at Betty's house in Santa Fe; his finding the lists of seventy-eight Seven members in the attic of the Holden house; his meeting with Jake in Tucson; the second break-in and ransacking of Betty's house; his and Jake's discovery of the summaries and photos Warren Holden had hidden in a secret compartment of a doghouse he had built; the clandestine driving trip around the west that Bill and Jake took to mail copies of the lists, summaries, and photos to seventy-six people on the lists, excluding only the late Colonel West and a made-up name that Warren Holden added to the list as a clue to where he hid the summaries and pictures; the revelation from the lists that members of The Seven included Ross Duncan, the Senate majority leader, as well as Robert Walker, the director of the CIA, and James Winston, the White House press secretary; that one of Jake's CIA source's brother-in-law was murdered after getting drunk and bragging about being a member of The Seven; the murder of Leon Jenkins, a Washington Post editor who was on the lists and was nervous and seen as a risk; the suicide of James Winston; that Larry Sullivan, Bill's secret Pentagon source, had warned him off The Seven and ended their relationship; the agreement among Bill, Jake, and Max to try to stop The Seven; and the fact that Max was being considered for the job of White House press secretary.

"Wow. That's a lot to digest. I knew about Winston's suicide, but I didn't know he was part of The Seven. And those mailings certainly explain why everyone seemed distracted and Snakebite was put on hold."

"It is a lot. I've been writing a kind of backward diary to try to make more sense out of it all. In fact, I was working on it when you knocked on the door last night. But it wasn't helping as much as I thought. Talking to you is far more valuable."

"For me, too. By the way, what was that comment you made about a fishing trip?"

"Oh, yeah. Duncan and Walker were supposedly on a fly-fishing trip together in New Mexico recently. I'll bet they were at that other secret Seven facility you mentioned."

"Probably."

"They must be fairly high in the hierarchy of The Seven. Given their powerful government positions, they could be on the board, so to speak. Jake and I considered confronting Duncan directly, but eventually decided to take West's advice and gather our forces first, working from the outside toward the center of power. We even set up what Jake called a 'button-down' security plan that would mean the release to the press of the stuff we earlier mailed plus the West letter and a summary of events I wrote if anything happened to either of us. I read online later that it's the same idea that is sometimes called a dead man's switch used by suicide bombers. The bomber has the switch down. If he's killed by a sniper, the switch is released, and the bomb goes off. Harm him or her and BOOM! But we canceled that when we decided not to confront Duncan."

"When will we know if Max Burris gets the White House job?"

"Today or tomorrow, I think. I'm having dinner with him and Jake tonight."

"How are we going to stay in touch since I left my cell phone in Maine?"

"We shouldn't say anything important on the phone anyway. Maybe we shouldn't even talk on the phone. But in case of an emergency, why don't you take my phone with you back to New York? I can always use Jake's or Max's."

"Okay."

"One more thing. I've made it clear to Max and Jake that our threesome would become four when you showed up. Do you have any problem with that?"

"Not at all. Count me in. I agree with West. The Seven must be stopped."

A few minutes later the Acela pulled into Union Station. Bill and Morgen hugged and kissed goodbye. Bill headed out to the street to get a taxi. Morgen looked at some magazines at a newsstand until the northbound train was announced.

CHAPTER 7

Only after Bill was settled into his room at the Hay-Adams did it dawn on him that if Max or Jake tried to call his cell phone, they would get Morgen. He used the hotel phone to dial Jake's cell.

"It's Bill. I just got here. At the Hay-Adams."

"I just got here myself. I'm at the usual place. With my ears open."

"I just wanted to let you know that I don't have my cell. I let someone borrow it. I'll explain everything at dinner." *Be careful with names and details over the phone. Jake was clearly also being cautious.*

"Why don't you set something up for dinner tonight and then let me know where and when. By the way, I have an extra cell phone you can use. It's a burner I got yesterday as a backup. You'll need it. One of us might have to reach you."

"Good point, I guess."

"Call me when you know about dinner."

"Will do. Bye."

Bill put the phone back in its cradle and started to turn on the television when the phone rang.

"Hello."

"Jesus, Bill. It's Me."

Bill immediately recognized Max's voice.

"I've been trying to reach you. I called your cell and someone else answered. They said you loaned them your cell phone." *Max is avoiding using names on the phone. He's hinting I should do the same.*

"I did. I figured I could use yours or a friend's. But I lined up another one I can use."

"Well, you're probably going to need it. Are you sitting down? I have some bad news?"

"What?"

"Larry Sullivan is dead. Murdered. His body was found by a jogger a couple of hours ago in an isolated area of Rock Creek Park. He had been shot in the back of the head, execution style. His hands were tied behind his back. The cops think he was killed somewhere else and dumped at the park. Probably last night."

"Oh, my God! This is terrible."

"I know. Look, we'll talk later."

"Can the three of us have dinner tonight?"

"Yes. Good idea."

"Where?"

"How about my apartment again. Is seven-thirty okay?"

"Yes, we'll be there."

"See you then."

Bill called Jake's cell. There was no answer. He left a message: "Our friend's apartment. Seven-thirty."

＊

Bill, Jake, and Max were sitting in Max's living room with its spectacular view of the Potomac River. On the dining room table were two bags of take-out Chinese food. They were sharing a bottle of Merlot.

Bill was clearly distraught.

"Larry's murder has got to be The Seven again. They did this because he was poking around about them. Something I asked him to do. I'm to blame for this."

Max held his hand in the air, palm out, toward Bill.

"Stop it, Bill. You can't blame yourself for what these murderous bastards do. The best thing we can do for ourselves and Sullivan is to follow our original plan and stop these fuckers. Hopefully before they kill anyone else."

"I know. You're right. But, Jesus. Larry Sullivan. I've known him a long time. He was the best source I ever had. Jake, you didn't know this, but Larry was my Pentagon source who helped me find Colonel West. He was also my source who was trying to find something on The Seven for me. He was the one who warned me to back off and drop The Seven. He said it was top secret and was being 'handled' by the military. He walked away and I never saw him again. He even changed his phone number so I couldn't call him."

"You told me that. I just didn't know his name."

Max spoke up.

"There'll be a story about his murder in tomorrow's Post and a lot of other places, I'm sure. It's already on D.C. radio and TV stations. What a fix for a reporter to be in. I know the real story but can't write it. Not yet, anyway."

"Do you know anything about Larry's family?" Bill asked. "I know he was married, but I never met his wife. I don't remember him ever saying anything about kids."

"I heard something on the radio about a wife. No mention of kids. I'll know more later. I'm not sure yet who's working the story. I'll try to have someone in the newsroom email it to be here as soon as its ready."

Bill looked at Jake.

"One thing that bothers me, though, is how Larry was killed. It doesn't fit the way we've seen The Seven operate, especially using cars."

Jake shrugged.

"Maybe they were trying to send a message. A brutal warning. But to whom?"

Following a few seconds of silence, Max spoke up.

"Before we go any further, I have some news. Jake, I think this is the first you're heard of this. You're having dinner tonight with the next White House press secretary."

"Congratulations," Bill and Jake both said at the same time as they stood up and shook Max's hand.

"When did you find out?" Bill asked.

"Not long after we talked this afternoon. Stanton called me. He's going to make the announcement at a press conference with me tomorrow afternoon."

Jake looked up.

"When will you start?"

"Right after the press conference. I talked to the executive editor and, of course, he said do what I had to do. No concern about two-week's notice or anything. He also said I would always be welcome back as long as he was there, which was nice. Of course, this will reflect pretty nicely on the Post. It also gives the paper a friend inside the Oval Office."

Max pointed to his dining room table.

"We'd better eat before the food gets cold. Sorry for red wine with Chinese food. I'm out of beer."

The conversation slowed as the three filled their plates with fried rice and moo shu pork, along with Mandarin pancakes and spring rolls.

Max was the first to take a pause from eating.

"Bill, when did Morgen return? When I tried to call your cell today, she answered."

Jake looked surprised.

"I didn't know Morgen had returned."

"I didn't want to tell you over the phone. You two have made me paranoid about phones. Then when we got here, we were occupied with Larry's murder and Max's news. But, yes, she has returned. I don't know for how long. She showed up at my apartment around eleven-thirty last night. She's been working for The Seven in Maine to discredit some academics who were getting too close to the truth. She said she had the feeling that The Seven people didn't really trust her, that they were always following her work a little too closely. But she said that all that stopped a couple of weeks ago. They were upset and distracted and seemed to have lost interest in her. This fits with what we picked up after the mailings arrived. She told them she needed to come to New York to take care of some family business, which was partly true. She needs to arrange to sell her father's house in the Bronx. But her main reason was to contact me. She got the same kind of letter from West that I did. West was right. She is disillusioned with The

Seven and wants to join us to try to stop it. She said there is no doubt they are planning a coup. She said she overheard it referred to as Operation Snakebite. She knows a lot about The Seven. She said they have two secret operational centers, one near Pine Bush, New York, the other in New Mexico. The one near Pine Bush is where she and I were taken when I met with West. Morgen was on the train with me to D.C. earlier today. She turned around and went back to New York. She's staying at my apartment. She left her cell in Maine, so I loaned her mine."

Jake reached into his pocket and pulled out a cell phone, which he handed to Bill.

"Here's the burner I mentioned. The number is taped to the back."

Jake wrote the number on a small piece of notebook paper and passed it to Max.

Max glanced at the paper, folded it, and put it in his shirt pocket. He picked at some food on his plate with a chopstick.

"What the hell am I supposed to do? Walk into the Oval Office tomorrow and tell Stanton that his CIA director and the Senate majority leader are planning a coup against the government? That his former press secretary was in on it? Is what we've got at this point enough proof? I don't think so."

"I don't think so, either," Jake said.

"Plus, I haven't really known Stanton all that long. I don't have a relationship or history with him like Jim Winston did. I need to work on building his confidence in me. Gaining his trust."

Max looked at Bill and then at Jake.

"There's something I still don't get. What's this coup all about? What's the point? Why does The Seven want to take over the United State government? How are they going to do it? What the hell does that have to do with UFOs and aliens? Are they worried that Stanton might expose them and tell the truth to the public? If they stage a coup, won't the public know what's going on?"

There was silence as Bill poured more wine.

Jake took a slow sip before he spoke.

"I think we may be missing something. Forest and trees kind of thing. We need to go back and look at the lists again. I mentioned this in passing to Bill some time ago, but a good many of these people Holden listed, especially members of Congress, have anti-government sentiments. Some of them— at least four or five, as I remember—are pushing secessionist movements in their home states. Almost all are in lock step with the NRA when it comes to guns and politics. What if their primary interest is not UFOs? What if they see The Seven, or what it has become, as a route to stage a coup? Maybe they want to use the power and resources of The Seven to establish a powerful authoritarian government more to their liking. One they could never realize through the democratic process. Maybe that's the real message in those lists. Maybe Holden created lists of people who were something of a fifth column within The Seven. Using it for their political ends."

"But West was included," Bill interrupted.

"I know. But maybe the colonel had his change of heart later. After all, despite his apparently sincere letter from the grave, remember what he helped orchestrate when you were in Indiana last year. Count the bodies."

"I have. Many times."

Max sighed and pulled his cell phone out of his pocket. He called the Post newsroom and asked an editor there to email him a copy of the Sullivan story when it was ready.

"It's more or less ready now," the editor said. "The copy desk is still fiddling with it, but not for anything major. Just coding. It's going on page one. Want me to send it now?"

"That would be great. Thanks."

In less than a minute, Max's phone beeped that an email was incoming. Max went into his office and printed out three copies. He gave one to Bill and another to Jake.

The story didn't tell them much new. The body was found by a jogger in Rock Creek Park. Larry, who was forty-five years old, was killed execution-style, hands tied behind his back and shot at close range in the back of his head. Police said they had no suspects. Robbery appeared not to be a motive. His wallet, with credit cards and two-hundred-thirty-six dollars in cash, was in his back pocket. He was a colonel stationed at the Pentagon, where he was assigned to an Army intelligence unit, and had told friends he planned to retire next year. He had been decorated for combat duty in the second Iraq war. His only other overseas duty was a stint in South Korea. A native of Oklahoma, he was survived by his wife, Judy, and his parents. He was an only child and he and his wife had no children.

Bill looked at Max.

"I know you say I shouldn't, but I still feel responsible for Larry's murder. If I hadn't sent him looking ...."

"There may be a bright spot in all this," Jake interrupted.

"How so?"

"Sullivan's murder may be a sign of how rattled the guys who run The Seven are. They're striking out blindly, it seems to me. It also is more evidence that they don't know what we're up to or that we were responsible for the mailings. Maybe we've overestimated how smart these guys are. Maybe the confusion we've created gives us an opening to get what we need: hard evidence. Documents. Recordings. Those lists and summaries, as well as the pictures, may go a long way toward proving the existence of The Seven. But not that the group is planning a coup. Even the letter from West could be explained away as the ravings of a sick, disgruntled man. Bill, you say Morgen has no doubt they are planning a coup. She said they call it Operation Snakebite. But we need real proof. Especially if Max tries to confront Stanton with this."

"So, what do we do next?" Bill asked. "Seem like we always come back to that question."

Jake paused before he replied.

"I think Morgen might be the key. She can work from the inside. Maybe find what we need. Or find someone who can and is willing. We all have to be careful. But maybe we have an advantage in that our proof doesn't have to be absolute. It only has to be strong enough to convince the President to move, but carefully. We know those lists are not all inclusive. We need to convince Stanton to form a small, working group of people he knows he can trust. We'll be telling him that the majority leader and the CIA director are traitors. Maybe others at a high level. We need enough evidence to make sure he believes us. Once Stanton is convinced, then we have the power and resources of the government behind us."

"I don't want to put Morgen in any danger."

"She's already in danger, especially if this outfit isn't stopped."

Max drummed his fingers on the dining room table.

"This is beginning to sound like a plan, but let's not get ahead of ourselves. Look, I've got to go to work at the White House for a man I don't have a longtime personal relationship with. I just can't go in there on the first day—or the first month or maybe the first six months—and confront him with all this. Not without ironclad proof. Maybe you're right, Jake. Maybe Morgen is the key. Maybe the four of us need to get together? How long is she going to be in New York?"

"I'm not sure, but certainly not longer than a few days. The Seven thinks she's in town to arrange to sell her dad's house in the Bronx. Which is true."

"Tomorrow's Friday. What if I came up on Sunday? Could you be there, Jake?"

"Sure."

"Then the four of us could meet at Bill's apartment and hash this out some more. Say noon? That seem reasonable?"

Bill and Jake nodded.

Before he left Washington on Friday, Bill used the phone Jake had given him to call George Carson, the chief doorman at Eastside Towers.

"George, it's Bill Sanders."

"Oh, Mr. Sanders. I didn't recognize your usual number."

"I'm using a friend's cell. George, would you do me a favor?"

"Sure. What is it?"

"Is Morgen in my apartment?"

"Yes. In fact, she went out earlier this morning and just returned a few minutes ago."

"George, could you tell her that I called you and that I'll be home in about three hours. And George, please go up to my apartment and tell her in person. Don't call her. I'll explain later."

"Whatever you say. No problem."

"Thanks, George."

Bill was back in New York by early afternoon. He took a taxi from Penn Station to his apartment on East Seventy-Second Street.

When he let himself in, the first thing he noticed was Morgen's perfume. She was sitting in the club chair reading a book.

"Welcome home."

Morgen stood and walked over toward Bill. She put her arms around his neck and kissed him.

"I missed you. How was D.C.? Anything new?"

"Yes. We have to talk. You want some water or coffee?"

"No. I'm good. You go ahead."

Bill walked into the kitchen and got a bottle of Evian water out of the refrigerator.

Bill and Morgen settled in the living room. Morgen returned to the club chair. Bill sat in the wingback.

"So, tell me."

"First, Max is going to be Stanton's new press secretary. In fact, there's going to be a White House press conference about it later this afternoon."

"That's great. That puts one of the four of us inside the White House."

"I know. But the problem is, Max and the President don't have a long relationship. They don't know each other that well. Max is going to have to figure out how to move fast. Because of the confusion our mailings caused, we have some time. But I don't think a lot."

"I agree."

"Max and Jake are coming to New York for a meeting with you and me at noon on Sunday. We have to make some plans. Jake thinks you might be able to work from the inside and find someone who's disillusioned and willing to talk or provide documents or recordings. Someone who can back up the documents we have and the letter from West. Jake and Max think we need another layer of proof if we go to Stanton."

"A month ago, I would have said that was impossible. Now, with what has happened with your mailings and the murders, I'm not so sure. I think a lot of people are rattled. Some may want out. This could give them the protection they need."

"Well, think about who it might be. What time is it?"

"Almost four."

Bill got up and turned on a wall-mounted television.

CNN had interrupted its regular programming to cover the White House news conference. Wolf Blitzer was speculating that Max would be named the President's new press secretary. *Hard to keep secrets in Washington.*

Suddenly, the press corps stood as President Stanton walked into the White House briefing room, Max at his side. Stanton was a commanding figure, tall and big with sharp features that some described as hawk-like.

He started by expressing sorrow over the death of Jim Winston and praising his work as press secretary. He then announced that, effective immediately, Max Burris would be the new top press aide.

"I really don't need to tell you much about Max," the President said. "You all know him well as one of the top reporters in Washington. I am fortunate he agreed to accept my offer."

Max then thanked the President and said he was looking forward to the challenges of the job.

The president took a couple of questions about Jim Winston's suicide. He repeated that he had no idea why Winston had killed himself. He answered a few more questions about a trade deal the United States was negotiating with China.

Max then took a few softball questions from the reporters.

The news conference ended after less than twenty minutes.

CNN then had a short interview with Max, who was wearing a dark suit and looked, Bill thought, less rumpled than usual. His intense dark eyes and graying black hair give him a professorial look. *The press will take him seriously, as it should. Will the President?*

Morgen clicked off the television.

"I have a surprise for you. I'm fixing dinner for the two of us here tonight. I went grocery shopping this morning. Hope you like linguini."

"I love it. I also love you."

Morgen got up and put her arms around Bill. She pulled him tight against her.

"I love you, too, Bill Sanders."

Bill and Morgen slept in Saturday morning. After a late breakfast, they decided to take advantage of the good weather and walk to the Metropolitan Museum of Art on Fifth Avenue to see an Edward Hopper exhibit.

"Since you cooked dinner last night, let's go out tonight. What are you in the mood for?"

"Let me think about it."

"Don't take too long. We have to make a reservation and it's Saturday. By the way, did you make any progress on your father's house?"

"I'm meeting a real estate agent Monday morning. I'll probably go back to Maine on Wednesday."

"Not for long, I hope."

"Me, too. God, Bill, will this nightmare ever be over?"

"All we can do is hope and try to make it happen."

Bill and Morgen held hands as they walked west toward Fifth Avenue.

While they were waiting to cross Fifth, Morgen turned to Bill.

"I've decided."

"About what?"

"Dinner tonight. French."

"Good idea. I know the place. Let me borrow my cell back for a minute."

He found Chez Maurice in his directory, called, and made a reservation for seven-thirty. Chez Maurice was a quiet little French restaurant Bill liked on the Upper East Side. It was where he and Jake had eaten when Jake came to New York several weeks ago.

＊

Sunday morning, Bill and Morgen were at Zabar's when it opened. They bought bagels, smoked salmon, roast beef, a loaf of garlic bread, and a loaf of rye bread. They also got some slaw and potato salad.

Back at the apartment, they prepared the dining room table for lunch.

At five after noon, the apartment phone rang. It was the weekend doorman.

"Mr. Sanders, there are two gentlemen here to see you."

"Send them up, please."

"Right away."

A few minutes later, there was a knock on the door. Bill opened it and welcomed Max and Jake into the apartment.

"Max, you know Morgen. Jake McCoy, Morgen Remley." They shook hands all around.

Bill pointed to the table.

"We have some deli food for lunch. Would you like wine, beer, or something else?"

"Wine," Max and Jake said almost in unison.

Bill went into the kitchen and pulled a bottle of Pinot Grigio from the refrigerator and lifted a bottle of Bordeaux from a small wine rack nearby.

"Please have a seat and help yourself. We can talk as we eat or wait until later. By the way, how was the trip up?

You took the train?"

Max smiled.

"Nope. When I told the President I had to come up here today to take care of some personal business, he insisted on sending me in a White House car with a driver who's a Secret Service agent. He's waiting in the car outside your building now. I told Stanton I was bringing a friend with me. He said no problem. I felt a little funny about it. I guess I'm not used to the perks of the job. But I'm working on it. I remember that a couple of past White House aides got in trouble for using government cars and helicopters for personal travel. I mentioned that to Stanton. He said that was before 9/11. Under new regulations, such trips can be authorized by the President if he thinks security is an issue."

After the four had settled down to lunch, Bill said that Morgen had agreed to work with them and would try to provide information from inside The Seven, as well as work to find someone they could turn who could provide crucial evidence they needed before confronting President Stanton.

Morgen nodded.

"I need to return to Portland on Wednesday, at the latest. One question I have is how we are going to stay in contact and communicate with one another. We can't use cell phones."

Jake smiled.

"I may be able to solve that problem. I'll know by tomorrow afternoon. If it works out, I'll come back up here Tuesday before Morgen has to leave. I'll explain the details to you and Bill then. I'll brief Max in D.C."

Bill looked at Jake.

"I hope whatever you come up with isn't too complicated. You know me and technology."

"Yeah, Flip-Phone Bill."

Everyone, including Bill, laughed.

After lunch, Bill made some coffee and their discussion turned more focused and serious.

"So, Jake, you're coming back up here on Tuesday with some way for us to communicate and keep private what we say among the four of us. Morgen will go back to Maine on Wednesday and try to gather more hard evidence. Max, you and Jake will drive back to D.C. this afternoon. At some point in the next few weeks—I may know exactly when this week—I have to fly out to Jefferson, Indiana, where Jack Turner and English-Frostmann are filming *Look Down*. I promised to be there because Turner's nephew, who is an Oscar-winning documentary film maker, wants to shoot a behind-the-scenes film about the making of the movie *Look Down*. He wants me there for interviews, and I've committed to do it. My agent, Nancy Luke, will be there with me. It shouldn't take longer than a week."

Jake stirred some sugar into a second cup of coffee.

"The problem for us right now is timing. We're pretty certain The Seven is confused and that Operation Snakebite, whatever it is, is on hold. But how long will it say that way? We don't know. A week? A month? We may have to move suddenly and quickly. Hopefully, Morgen will be able to help us with this."

"I'll do my best."

Max pushed his empty coffee cup aside and looked around the table.

"There's still something I don't understand. Assume The Seven is planning a coup against the United State government. How the hell do they pull it off? I mean, come on. I don't care how pervasive or powerful The Seven is, we're talking about the U.S. government. The military. Hundreds of thousands of well-armed soldiers with access to all kinds of sophisticated weapons and aircraft. Even nuclear weapons, for Christ's sake. Is The Seven powerful enough to take them on? Or is this just some kind of crazy conspiracy theory brewing in the dark corners of the Internet? Some QAnon fantasy? Are we overreacting? Fighting shadows?"

There were several seconds of silence around the table. Jake broke it.

"I don't think so. For several reasons. There have been too many bodies. The old hands I've talked to from Langley, the ones I really trust, are convinced that something big is in the works. Your point about the power of the government and the military is well taken, but remember where power really rests in our system. At the top. The structure is top down. If The Seven made a series of surgical strikes that took down the non-Seven D.C. power structures and coupled that with some spectacular event like 9/11 that horrified and scared people and diverted their attention, it could be done. Look at those lists we have. The majority leader, the director of the CIA. Three Secret Service agents guarding the President. The President's press secretary. It goes on and on. And we know those lists only scratch the surface. What about the Vice-President? The Speaker of the House? The Joint Chiefs? Democracy is fragile. A big part of its survival depends on a gentlemen's agreement to do the right thing, to play by the rules—even if sometimes they're customs, not laws. Without that, as we have seen various times in the past, the foundation is weak. I think The Seven is a real threat. The key to stopping it is to strike first. That's why timing is so important. We need to hit them before they try something. Afterward will be too late."

On Monday morning, while Morgen was meeting with her real estate agent, Bill called Bob Bowers, his lawyer.

"Bob, can we get together this week and deal with the will thing?"

"Sure. In fact, I just had a cancellation. Can you come by in an hour?"

"That would be perfect. See you then. Thanks."

Bill was pretty sure he'd be back before Morgen, but just in case he left a note on the dining room table explaining where he was.

Bowers greeted Bill in the reception area of his office. They walked together down a hallway to Bob's expansive wood-paneled office overlooking Third Avenue.

"Coffee?"

"Sure."

Bob walked over to a kitchenette in the corner of his office and poured two mugs of steaming coffee.

"Sugar? Cream?"

"Just cream."

Bob sat at his desk. Bill took a Windsor chair that was angled in front of the desk.

"I kept that sealed envelope in my safe like you instructed."

"Thanks, Bob. Hang on to it for a while longer. I'll pick it up at some point."

"And tell me what the hell you've been up to."

"Yes, but not yet."

"Well, let's get your will put in order. If you kicked off now, it'd be a hell of a mess. You left everything to Jane. Heck, the state would probably wind up with most of it. You've got a lot of money for a poor farm kid from ... Kentucky?"

"Indiana, mainly."

"And you don't have any relatives?"

"Not really. Some distant cousins I don't even know."

"So, who do you want to leave your property and money to? What about Jane's family?"

"She was an only child, and both her parents are dead."

"Who, then?"

"I've been thinking about that. If something happens to me, sell the apartment. Combine that money with my other funds and leave it all, except for a hundred thousand dollars, to Indiana University to establish full four-year scholarships for minority students in the name of Daniel Scott."

"Who's Daniel Scott?"

"I never knew him. Oddly enough, I saw him only once. After he was dead. Murdered. He was a young, black reporter for the Jefferson Courier in my hometown of Jefferson, Indiana. It's a tangled story. But if I hadn't shown up, he might still be alive. His parents live in Denver. They should be notified of this in the event of my death. I want you to call them personally. I'll get their names and phone number for you."

"You're not making much sense, Bill. What about the

hundred thousand?"

"I want to leave that to the daughter of a cleaning lady who was killed last year in Santa Fe. I'll get you her name and address later this week. Remember Senator Warren Holden?"

"Vaguely."

"The cleaning lady worked for him and his wife, Betty. She was killed when their home was broken into not long after Warren's death."

"Did you know the cleaning lady or her daughter?"

"No."

"This is weird. You want to leave your money for a scholarship fund named after a dead guy you never met and the daughter of a dead cleaning lady you didn't know."

"That about sums it up."

"What if you get married again? How likely is that?"

"Not likely at the moment. But if I do, I can always change the will."

"Yes, you can. Okay, let me get to work on this. I'll have to figure out some structure for the scholarships for you to approve. Do you want to give I.U. a lot of autonomy in running the fund, or do you want to set conditions for it?"

"Let the university run it. The only conditions I want is that that the scholarships go to low-income minority students and be named for Daniel Scott."

"That should be fairly easy to set up."

"Good. I'll be in touch in a day or so with those addresses and phone numbers."

Bill arrived back at the apartment shortly after one. As soon as he walked in, the phone started ringing. It was Nancy Luke.

"Hey, Nancy. What's up?"

"Can we have lunch on Wednesday? I know it's off our regular schedule, but we need to discuss some things."

"Sure. At one?"

"Yes. See you then. Call me Wednesday morning to double confirm."

"Okay."

Morgen returned a few minutes after he finished talking to Nancy. They shared food left over from Sunday and finished the bottle of Pinot Grigio.

Sunlight was streaming in the south window, highlighting Morgen's blond hair. She looked at Bill.

"I'm ready for a nap."

"Are you sleepy?"

"Do I look sleepy?"

She started to unbutton her blouse, took Bill's hand, and pulled him toward the bedroom.

That evening Bill and Morgen walked to the nearby Italian restaurant that Bill liked.

After the wine was poured, Bill reached across the table and took Morgen's hand.

"We haven't had any time to talk. How was your meeting with the real estate agent? Did you get anything started or settled?"

"Sort of. The tenants who are living there have a lease that runs for six more months. They were planning to move then anyway, so getting them out won't be a problem. They're very nice, actually. They allowed me and the agent to do a walk-through of the house. Susan—that's the agent's name—said the house needed some minor repairs and cosmetic work before she could put it on the market. She'll take care of that as soon as the renters are out. The work shouldn't take more than a month or two. What did you do this morning?"

"Talked to my lawyer, Bob Bowers. He's reworking my will. I hadn't changed it since Jane died. I don't have any relatives. Unless my life changes, I'm leaving almost everything to Indiana University to establish a scholarship fund in the name of Daniel Scott."

"Isn't he the reporter who was killed last year in Indiana?"

"Yes. The fine work of The Seven. I'm also leaving some money to the daughter of Warren and Betty Holden's cleaning lady, who was also killed by The Seven last year during the break-in at their house I told you about. I somehow feel responsible, especially in the case of Daniel Scott. If I hadn't stirred things up in Jefferson, he might still be alive."

"What about your friend, Paul?"

"It's complicated. I guess I don't think of him as an innocent bystander, although he was a victim. He was headed down a self-destructive path with booze. Understandable but self-destructive, nevertheless. Think of it. Plagued by those 'memory attacks' of his own childhood abductions and then witnessing his daughter abducted the same way. Who the hell wouldn't reach for the bottle?"

"That's one of the reasons I love you, Bill Sanders. You consider other people."

"What's going to happen to us, Morgen? What if The Seven can't be stopped. Does that doom us?"

A tear slid down Morgen's cheek. Bill wiped it away with his hand.

"I don't know. I sometimes fantasize that we can run away from it all. Flee the country. Hide out someplace. But I know that would never work. We have to see this through, Bill. I know The Seven too well. It's our only hope.

Tuesday morning, before he had even gotten out of bed, the burner phone Jake had given Bill beeped that a text message had been received. Bill turned on his bedside light and picked up the phone. The message was from Jake. The text simply said: 2 p.m.

Bill rolled over and kissed Morgen's neck.

"Hmmm ... what time is it?"

"It's almost eight. I just got a text from Jake. He'll be here at two."

"Then we've got plenty of time."

Morgen pulled Bill against her and stretched, pressing her body against his. Bill reached over and clicked off his bed-side light.

Later in the morning, Bill and Morgen were having coffee and cereal at the dining room table. They were still wearing robes.

"How come you didn't tell me that Nancy Luke was going to Indiana with you?"

"I didn't think it was important. Why? Are you jealous?"

"Should I be?"

"Of course not. You know better. Nancy and I are strictly business. Also, she's married to one of the richest lawyers in New York."

"I do know better. I'm just teasing you. I'm in a good mood. Sex is a great way to start the day."

"Sure is."

✳

Jake knocked on the apartment door a little after two.

Bill opened the door. Jake was carrying a canvas tote bag.

"Welcome. Come in. Do you want anything to drink or eat?"

"No, thanks. I had some lunch on the way."

"You took the train?"

"No. I rented a car and drove. I didn't want to risk any security encounters over what I'm carrying."

"Where'd you park?"

"Your buddy, George, remembered me and said he'd take care of it. I'm supposed to call him when I'm ready to leave and he said he'd have the car out front."

"There's a parking garage under this building. The entrance is around to the side."

Jake walked over the dining room table and set the tote bag on it. He reached in and pull out what looked like two Apple iPhones and two Apple watches and chargers to match them.

Morgen came out of the bedroom.

"Hi, Jake."

"Morgen. How are you today?"

"Good, thanks. What's with the iPhones?"

"Well, if you look closely, you'll notice that these iPhones are a little thicker than they should be. Not much. But a little. They're also a bit heavier. You'll understand why as I explain them."

Bill looked pained.

"Relax, Bill. They're simple to use."

"I hope so."

"Here's the deal. There are four of these phones and matched watches. I have mine. I gave Max his yesterday. These two sets are yours. You can use them like a regular phone to make a regular call using a cellular signal, except they don't have a number. No one can call you. If you call someone, their caller ID will simply say caller unknown or something like that, depending on their service provider. They recharge just like regular phones and watches.

"Taped to the back of each of these phones and watches is a single number, either one, two, three, or four. Those numbers are assigned to the four of us alphabetically. Bill is one, I'm two, Max is three, and Morgen is four. Each phone is programmed to call the other three when you simply push the number of the phone you want to call. If I want to call Morgen, I press four. The phone won't ring. A little green light will indicate an incoming call and the single number of the caller will appear. In addition to the light, the watch you'll be wearing is linked to your phone and will vibrate for an incoming call. The single number of the called will also appear on the watch face. If you can't answer the call right then, you know who to call back.

"Here's an interesting part. These phones don't use cellular signals to communicate with each other. Instead, they use the Internet. So, you have to be in range of WiFi for your phone to work. If a WiFi signal is password protected, your phone will automatically override the password and work anyway. And you're invisible to the WiFi owner. If one of us tries to call you and you're not connected to WiFi, the single number associated with the caller will show up on your watch face, along with the time and date. That's a signal to find some WiFi and call back. Another thing: If any one of us punches the number nine, it causes that number to be displayed on all the other phone screens and the watch faces. That's a signal for the others to also punch nine within two minutes. That will link us into a conference call. If one of us is in a meeting or something and can't respond by pressing nine, the conference call will be among the other three.

"Now here's the best part. These phones totally encrypt outgoing and incoming conversations among us. I mean totally. If somebody manages to intercept a call, all they will hear is gobbledygook. If you call someone else using a cellular signal, the conversation won't be scrambled.

"When you take your phone and watch, remove the numbers taped to their backs. Since these number are linked to our first names alphabetically and there are only four of us, these should be no problem. Right, Bill?"

"I'll do my best."

Morgen smiled and took Bill's hand in hers.

Jake then pulled his phone, number two, out of his jacket pocket.

"Let's have a little practice. Bill, call me."

Bill released Morgen's hand, picked up his phone, number one, and pressed the number two on the keypad. In seconds, Jakes green light blinked on and the number one appeared on his screen. He held up his left hand. His watch was gently vibrating and the number one appeared on its face.

Jake swiped an icon and answered the phone.

"This is a test," he said.

"Did I pass?" Bill replied.

"With flying colors."

Morgen looked directly at Jake.

"Jake, this is amazing. Where in the name of God did you get these things on such short notice?"

"I was a CIA field agent for most of my working life. I have friends in low places."

It was almost four when Jake said he had to leave to drive back to Washington.

"I know I'm going to hit heavy traffic, but I need to get back tonight. I'm flying home to Tucson tomorrow morning. Morgen, you're going back to Maine tomorrow, right?"

"Yes. I think my flight leaves a little after one."

"Well, we'll be in a holding pattern for a few days until we know what you can find out in Maine. I can come back to D.C. or here on a moment's notice if I have to. Max needs some time to settle in with his new job. Bill, you have to figure out when you're going to Indiana. We'll stay in touch."

After Jake had left, Morgen looked at Bill.

"What do you want to do for dinner tonight?"

"I don't know. What do you want?"

"Why don't we order Chinese and stay in. It could be our last night together for a while."

"I like the way you think."

Chapter 8

Ross Duncan, the Senate majority leader, and Robert Walker, the director of the CIA, sat together on a park bench overlooking the Tidal Basin. Their government limousines were parked nearby. Six plainclothes security agents were standing in the background, creating a half circle around the two. The agents were close enough to act if they were needed but far enough away that they couldn't hear what Duncan and Walker were saying.

Walker was pointing his right index finger at Duncan.

"I still don't understand why we had to kill that colonel at the Pentagon. What was his name?"

"Sullivan. Larry Sullivan."

"I mean what the hell did he exactly do that got you so upset?"

"Last year, he inquired about West. Said he was looking for him on behalf of a distant cousin. We gave him the benefit of the doubt. Then a few weeks ago he started poking around about The Seven. We scared him off, but I didn't like it."

"Why was he asking about The Seven?"

"I'm not sure. My best guess is that somebody on one of those lists that were mailed panicked and talked to him."

"Could he have been asking on behalf of someone else? If so, why didn't we just kidnap him and force him to tell us. You know we could. We have experts in that area."

"That would have been too messy. We would still have had to kill him. It was my decision to eliminate him the way we did. I don't think he was acting for anyone. Anyway, what if he was? If there was somebody, I'll bet they've lost interest after hearing what happened to Sullivan. I wanted to clean it up quick. We don't have a lot of time, and things are starting to fray at the edges over those mailings. If Snakebite is going to succeed, we have to act soon. Maybe within a month. Can we move that quickly?"

"I think so. But we've got to get to the people on those lists and tighten things up. That State Department drunk who was blabbing about The Seven was a one-off. He was one of ours, but he wasn't on any of the lists. Jenkins at the Post was. We don't want a repeat of that. Hopefully, his demise put a scare into others on the lists. But we need to be sure."

"That shouldn't be hard. I'll get our guys working on it. They'll contact each one personally."

Duncan squinted and turned his head slightly to avoid the direct rays of the midmorning sun.

"Bob, what about the White House? Any problems there? Winston's suicide left a hole there that we can't easily or quickly fill. What about Stanton? Does he suspect anything?"

"I'm pretty sure he doesn't. He called me a while back and complained that he had a feeling some unspecified 'things' were being kept from him. He then asked about a final report on those Navy UFO sightings. I assured him all was well. He said he was probably just overtired and was flying to Camp David to relax for the weekend. I've known him for a long time and can tell you for a fact that he has no real interest in UFOs or aliens. He won't have a clue what's happening until it's too late."

"Good. That's one thing we don't have to worry about."

CHAPTER 9

Late Wednesday morning, Bill arranged for a car to take Morgen to LaGuardia for her flight to Portland. He was planning to ride to the airport with her, but she insisted he stay at the apartment and get back to his writing. She returned his cell phone and then stuck the new one that Jake had given her, number four, into her purse. She strapped the Apple watch on her left wrist. She was standing in the living room of Bill's apartment.

"I'm as ready as I'll ever be, I guess."

"Morgen, I don't want you to go."

"I don't want to go either. But you know I have to. We have to see this through for things to work out for us."

"I know."

Bill pulled her close to him and kissed her. She started to cry a little, and Bill touch her wet cheek with his fingers. He inhaled the musky scent of her perfume.

They embraced again in front of the apartment building after Bill had put her suitcase in the car's trunk. She waved from the back seat as the car pulled out into the Seventy-Second Street traffic.

It was shortly after eleven when Bill returned to his apartment. He was lonely and angry. *The fucking Seven has done nothing but fuck up my life.* Then he had a twinge of guilt. *I should be grateful that at least I have a life. Larry Sullivan! This has to stop.*

The sudden ringing of his home phone broke his mood. He glanced at the caller ID. Nancy Luke.

"Hello, Nancy."

"Bill, I haven't heard from you. Are we still on for lunch today?"

SECRETS

"Oh, I'm sorry. I was so tied up with things here that I forgot all about it. I'm really sorry. But yes, for sure. One, right?"

"Yes, see you then."

"Right. Bye."

✳

Nancy was already seated at their usual table at Dave's when Bill arrived.

"You're looking perky, Bill. Work must be going well."

"It is. I'm a little behind schedule but catching up. But remember, I still will likely have to take some more time off in the coming weeks. I'm sure glad you put that six-month extension clause in my contract."

Gerald, their usual waiter, interrupted to take their drink orders. Both ordered iced tea.

"What's up, Nancy?"

"A couple of things. I've had several conversations with Jack Turner. Looks like his nephew, Richard Turner, wants you to be in Jefferson a week from today for interviews for his documentary. Jack won't start filming until a couple of weeks later, but apparently Richard wants to get the parts with you in the can before he does the rest."

"I guess that'll work. Are you still going out there with me?"

"Yes. Turns out that my husband will be in China on business for most of the next month, so the timing is perfect."

"I'll try to get us reservations at the Jefferson Hotel, but it may be all booked up. Graham Neal, the owner of the Jefferson Courier, has offered to let us stay at his house, which is plenty big enough."

"It's all taken care of. Jack arranged for us to have rooms at the hotel."

"We're still flying out there in the studio plane?"

"Yes. We leave at ten in the morning a week from today. We can take a car together to Teterboro."

Gerald returned to take their lunch orders. Both had Cobb salads.

81

"What's the other thing?"

"Brace yourself. Jack and English-Frostmann won't announce this for another week, but guess who's going to play the adult Joseph in *Look Down*?"

"You know?"

"Yep. Jack told me but swore me to secrecy. But I don't think he'd mind if I told you. You wouldn't blab it to anyone, would you?"

"Of course not. You know me better than that."

"Yes, I do. Well, it's Brett Cooper. The young Joseph will be played by Simon Carey."

"Wow! That's great. Both top box-office draws. Especially Brett Cooper. Will they be in Jefferson when we are?"

"I'm not sure. You may have to go back if you want to meet them."

"I just might."

Gerald arrived with their salads.

As they were finishing lunch, Nancy's tone turned serious.

"Bill, are you making any progress dealing with those events in Indiana last year? Has there been any word on your friend's daughter?"

"Not yet. Not really. But I'm still involved. I know I told you I would explain it all to you at some point, and I will. Maybe on the flight to Jefferson, depending on events."

"Whatever works for you, Bill."

CHAPTER 10

Cecil Perkins, the White House Chief of Staff, left the Oval Office for his own nearby West Wing office after briefing the President on the latest budget impasse in the Senate. It was almost two o'clock.

President Stanton got up from his desk and walked across the room. He stood near the fireplace for a few minutes, deep in thought.

He walked back to his desk and picked up the phone.

"Yes, Mr. President?"

"Martha, I think my schedule is clear for the next hour. Right?"

"Yes, Sir. But we kept it clear so you could go to the residence and rest for a bit. Remember what the doctor said about too much stress."

"I know. I know. But I need that hour today. Connect me with Max Burris. And can you have Adalberto bring coffee for two."

"Right away, Sir."

There was a click followed by a moment of silence.

"Hello, Sir."

"Max, can you come into my office for a few minutes?"

"Be right there."

A Secret Service agent stationed near Martha's desk opened the curved door to the Oval Office for Max.

The President looked up from a paper he was reading at his desk.

"Come in, Max."

The President got up and motioned for Max to follow him

to the pair of blue and gold sofas in front of the fireplace. The President sat in a wingback chair; Max settled into the end of one of the sofas nearest the chair.

Adalberto, a White House steward, entered the Oval Office from a door that connected to a small kitchen. Without saying a word, he sat a tray containing a silver carafe of coffee, two White House cups and saucers, and a silver bowl of sugar and a small matching silver pitcher of cream. There was also a plate of sugar cookies.

"Thank you, Adalberto."

The steward nodded to the president and left the room.

The President poured a cup of coffee and pushed it toward Max.

"Help yourself, Max. You like it black, as I remember."

He poured a second cup for himself and added a generous amount of cream.

"Max, I've been meaning to talk with you for a couple of days now."

"What about, Sir?"

"Well, you've only been working here a little more than two weeks, but you're doing a hell of a job. You're very good at framing things to the press in such a way that it not only puts me in a good light but actually represents what I think and what I'm trying to do."

"Thank you, Sir."

"But there's another reason I wanted to talk. I'm pretty good at reading people, at picking up vibes. It's a skill that helped get me this job and get reelected. I'm also pretty good at knowing when someone is lying to me, or when they're trying to kiss my ass just because I'm the President. I don't sense either of those in your case. I think you're a straight shooter. But I do get the sense sometimes that you're holding something back that you'd like to tell me. I had a similar feeling about Jim Winston for about a year before he died. I'd known him for years, but something changed toward the end. He became somewhat distant, and I had the nagging feeling that he wanted to tell me something, but he couldn't bring himself to do it. Then he killed himself. I guess I'll never know."

"Mr. President, are you trying to ask me something? Or tell me something?"

"Maybe. While I don't think you're lying or pandering, I have to make up my mind if I fully trust you like I fully trusted Jim Winston until the last year."

"Sir, if you can't fully trust me, I shouldn't be in this job. You should never have hired me."

"You're right. You know, when we did a background check on you, even your ex-wife sang your praises. How long have you been divorced?

"A little over five years."

"Well, I just decided I do trust you. Sit still for a minute. I want to show you something."

The president got up and walked over to his desk. First, he pressed the left button under the edge of his desk that turned off all audio and video recordings in the Oval Office. Then he took a key from his pocket and unlocked a drawer on the bottom right. He retrieved a White House envelope, carried it back to the seating area, and handed it to Max. On the outside of the envelope, in handwritten capital letters, were four words: THE PRESIDENT. EYES ONLY.

"What's this?"

"Look inside."

Max lifted the envelope's flap and pull out a folded sheet of White House stationery. He opened it out. In the center were five handwritten lines, also in capital letters:

THE SEVEN
ROSS DUNCAN
ROBERT WALKER
THREE SS
SNAKEBITE

Max couldn't believe what he was seeing. He had to fight to keep his hand from shaking.

The President took a sip of coffee.

"Does this mean anything to you?"

"Where did you get this, Mr. President?"

"Right after I returned from Jim's funeral in Cleveland, Martha, my secretary, was cleaning out his desk—now your desk—and found it. It's Jim's handwriting. I know who Duncan and Walker are. What the hell is The Seven? And Snakebite? And Three SS?"

"Who else has seen this?"

"Just the two of us."

"Sir, how private are we right now?"

"Pretty private. Before I got the envelope out of the desk, I switched the Oval to dark. No voice or video recordings."

"Are you sure?"

"I have no reason to think otherwise. How private do you want to be?"

"Totally. In fact, I'd feel better talking to you outside in the middle of the South Lawn. Or in the woods at Camp David."

"Max, what the hell are you saying? Do you know what Jim's list means? Why all the secrecy?"

"Sir, if you trust me, don't push me on this right now. There is a group of four people—three others and me—that you need to meet with. That meeting has to be in total secrecy. Not a word about it to anyone. Not the Chief of Staff. Not your secretary. No one. We can't meet here. The White House is too public. Maybe Camp David. Your presidency and the country may depend on how seriously you take this. The reason I don't want to go into it now is that I don't have the evidence that will convince you. You will see it when you meet with the group. But in the meantime, there's something you must do. Do you trust Ben Watkins, the director of the Secret Service?"

"Of course. Why wouldn't I?"

"Well, he needs to be a part of this, part of the group. That's because 'Three SS' stands for three Secret Service agents. They are traitors in your midst, Sir. I don't have their names right now, but I can get them. Before we can meet or do anything, those three have to be moved out of the White House. Transfer them. Promote them. Whatever it takes. But they cannot be aware of your movements and contacts."

"What do I tell Ben?"

"I don't know. But we can't bring him into our confidence until the three agents are gone. He has to get rid of those three agents before you, and he, can meet with this group."

"Max, this seems pretty wild. You're asking me to do a lot on faith in you."

"I know, Sir. But you have that list from Jim. It's not a joke."

"I guess you're right."

The President turned and glanced up at the portrait of Thomas Jefferson to the left of the fireplace.

CHAPTER 11

When Max returned to his office, he shut the door and pulled the special phone Jake had given him out of his pocket. He started to punch the one button that would connect him to Bill, but he hesitated and put the phone back in his pocket.

He picked up the receiver on his desk phone.

"Yes, Sir?"

"Sally, I'll be out of the office for about half an hour or so. Just take a message if anyone calls. If it's really important you can always page me."

"No problem."

Max left the West Wing through a little used side entrance. He put on a pair of sunglasses and walked over to the Pennsylvania Avenue side of the Eisenhower Executive Office Building. He continued for a block or so until he spotted a park bench that was empty. He sat down and pulled out Jake's phone. He was in a WiFi hot spot. He glanced around and pressed one.

"Hey, Max. What's up?"

"Where are you?"

"In my apartment in New York. Why?"

"We have to meet soon. I just had a talk with the President. Jim Winston left him a cryptic note with hints to The Seven. I've convinced him he needs to meet with the four of us and also bring the Secret Service director into the loop. But first we have to deal with those three White House agents that are on Holden's lists. Stanton has agreed to have them transferred or promoted, or something. I'm not sure how long that will take. And it has to be done in such a way as not to arouse The

Seven's suspicions. So, we can't just move all three at once. One at a time, over a period of time. Anyway, I don't have a copy of the lists and don't remember their names. Can you give them to me?"

"Sure. Hold on."

In a couple of minutes Bill returned to the phone and gave Max the three names. Max wrote them in a reporter's notebook he always carried.

"Max, when and how are we going to meet? Morgen's in Maine, and Jake is in Tucson."

"Jake's not a problem. Can't Morgen come back to New York because she has to deal with problems selling her father's house?"

"Maybe. Let me contact them both and get back to you with a good time. Given the demands of your job, a Sunday might be better."

"Yes, it would."

"We'll meet at my apartment?"

"Good idea. Get back to me as soon as you have a tentative arrangement. Best to call me at home at night. If I can't talk for some reason, I'll get right back to you."

"Hopefully, I'll know something by tonight."

✳

It was almost eleven before Bill called Max at his Watergate apartment.

"How about this Sunday at two at my apartment. Jake and Morgen are good to go. Morgen actually needs to come back to New York to approve some of the work on her father's house, as well as sign some papers and contracts. She says it's no problem with her Seven contacts."

"Great. I'll be there. I may have some more news. Stanton and I have a couple of meetings scheduled before then. He's going to press me for more information, but I'm going to insist he has to meet with us to get it. And we can't meet with him until those three agents are gone."

"I agree. But I have to go out to Indiana on Wednesday. I should be there for a week, perhaps a little less."

"Maybe by the time you get back the problem of the three agents will be solved, and we can set up a meeting with Stanton. But we've got to have harder evidence than we do now. We'll talk about it on Sunday."

"Okay. See you then."

＊

Morgen flew to New York on Saturday. She and Bill had dinner at a Spanish restaurant not far from Bill's apartment. They ordered sangria and grilled sausage for an appetizer. For the main course, they decided to share a seafood paella.

After the waiter had poured their sangrias and left the pitcher on their table, Morgen looked at Bill and smiled.

"I may have some good news."

"What?"

"I may have at least a piece of the proof we need, or Max needs, for the President."

"What is it? How did you manage that?"

"Well, I went out for drinks and dinner last week with a guy who works in my group in Portland. His name is Tom. We're not supposed to socialize, but with the confusion and distraction you and Jake caused, we figured no one would notice. He sometimes flirts with me, but in a very innocent way. He's only been out of college a couple of years. He couldn't find work and signed on with The Seven after a series of interviews. I gathered from hints he dropped that he wasn't too happy with the way things were working out. It turns out that his best friend from college also took a job with The Seven, at that compound in New Mexico. Like the one near Pine Bush. His friend is a computer whiz. In fact, he took the job so he could work with the advanced supercomputers in both places, something he would normally never get a chance of doing with only an undergraduate degree and at his age. Anyway, he was working one day not long ago when Ross Duncan and

Bob Walker flew there in separate military helicopters for a meeting. The friend doesn't know who else was there, but I think it was a meeting of The Seven. The directors, so to speak. Duncan and Walker must be the top dogs. The computer whiz was able to access and copy the helicopters' flight data and their manifests. Duncan was on the first helicopter that landed. In addition to the pilot and co-pilot, there was also a security guard on board who got off with Duncan. The second helicopter carrying Walker landed a few minutes later. There were two security guards on that flight; they also got off with Walker. Tom's friend mailed a copy of the data and manifests on a flash drive to Tom at his parents' house to avoid prying eyes of The Seven. Tom gave them to me."

"What's the date when Duncan and Walked flew there?"

"It's the same time they were supposed to be on a fly-fishing trip together in New Mexico."

"Morgen, that's incredible. That puts two very important guys on the lists in one of The Seven's lairs. Why did the computer whiz send that information to his friend? You have it with you?"

'I think he's very nervous about things he's seeing and hearing. He's also scared. I think he knows he's in over his head. One thing your mailings did was show that The Seven is not as airtight as it—and we—think it is. Those mailings were like an X-ray of a body: They showed weak spots in the bones. Jenkins at the Post was one. So was Jim Winston at the White House. And Tom. And the computer whiz in New Mexico. And, yes, I have the printouts with me. They're in my suitcase back at the apartment."

"Do we know the computer whiz's name?"

"No, but I can find out when I get back to Maine."

"Might be a good thing for us to know."

By two-thirty Sunday afternoon, Bill, Morgen, Max, and Jake were gathered around Bill's dining room table.

Morgen told the group what she had told Bill at dinner about how she got the data and manifests from New Mexico. Earlier in the day she had made photocopies, so they each had their own copy.

Jake looked over his glasses at the other three.

"This is incredible. This doesn't tell us what we need to know about Snakebite, but it sure as hell is proof of The Seven and a conspiracy. It's also proof that both Duncan and Walker lied when they said they were going fishing. Combined with the West letter and the other stuff we have, this ought to be enough to convince the President. What do you think, Max?"

"I think you're right. But first we have to deal with those three Secret Service agents currently assigned to the White House before we meet with the President. He's been working with Ben Watkins. He's the Secret Service director. But it's going to take some time—maybe a couple of weeks. It has to be done so as not to raise any red flags. I'll know more tomorrow when I have a meeting with Stanton and Watkins. By the way, the President, at my urging, wants Watkins included in our group. Also, a lifelong friend of Stanton's who is an Air Force colonel working for the Defense Intelligence Agency. His name is Cole Favate. I don't know him but assured Stanton it would be fine with all of us. It's hard to say no to a President, especially this one."

Jake turned toward the others.

"I agree with having the Secret Service director in. I've heard of Favate but don't know him. Everything I've heard about him is good. I recommend we trust Stanton on this."

The others nodded their heads in agreement.

Bill drummed his fingers on the table.

"Well, I'm heading out to Indiana on Wednesday for about a week. Morgen is returning to Maine on Tuesday. Maybe by the time I get back we'll be able to meet with Stanton, Watkins, and Favate. You all realize, don't you, that our group of four is about to become a group of seven?"

＊

Sunday evening, Bill and Morgen were alone in the apartment. Jake was on his way to the airport to catch an evening flight to Phoenix. Max was on his way back to Washington.

"Morgen, I didn't mean to speak for you when I told the others you were leaving Tuesday. I just assumed it because I'm leaving Wednesday. You can stay here as long as you need. You know that."

"Of course. But I am probably going to leave on Tuesday. I'll know tomorrow after I meet with Susan—the real estate agent—and see what all I have to do. Hopefully, I'll know in time to get a reservation to Portland on Tuesday."

"So that gives us two nights before we have to leave."

"Yep."

"Where do you want to go for dinner tonight?"

"How about we raid your refrigerator and stay in?"

CHAPTER 12

Bill and Nancy Luke were sitting opposite one another in the English-Frostmann jet. They were about halfway through the flight from Teterboro to Jefferson. Soon after they took off, the co-pilot had offered them a bottle of wine and a plate of cheese and snacks.

Bill reached for a cracker.

Nancy's eyes widened.

"Is that an Apple watch you're wearing? I never thought I'd see the day. It took ages to get you into a smart phone."

"A friend gave it to me. It's taking some getting used to. I'm trying to embrace more technology, but a little at a time. So, I guess I'll always be behind the curve."

Nancy sometimes teased Bill over his aversion to modern electronic devices. He often countered by reminding her of how little she knew of the United States outside of New York and California. Both were running jokes between them.

"Nancy, have you ever spent much time in the Midwest?"

"Outside of Chicago, no. I know it's a bit rude and snobby to say, but for me it's always been what they call flyover country."

"Well, Jefferson and Indiana are about as Midwest as you can get. You'll enjoy it. I'm also anxious for you to meet Graham Neal."

"The editor you once worked for, right?"

"Yes. A very smart guy and a good newsman."

"Bill, when are you going to explain all that Indiana stuff to me that started when you came out here last year to help your friend?"

Bill looked to the front of the plane. The door to the cockpit was closed.

"I know I said I might do it on the flight out today, but some things have come up, and I have to wait a while longer. I will tell you what I know, but just not now. I can tell you this. One of the main reasons I can't tell you now is that there are actually some government and national security issues involved. I need to get those resolved. Please just trust me."

"You know I do. But now you've whetted my appetite, as they say. How can national security be involved in the disappearance of a ten-year-old girl?"

"I just can't go into it now. But I promise I will. Probably soon. Maybe in a few weeks."

"Okay, mystery man. I'll wait. Does Jefferson have decent restaurants?"

*

When Bill and Nancy got their luggage out of their rental car and checked into the Jefferson Hotel, there were two messages waiting for Bill.

One was from Richard Turner: "Mr. Sanders, I had to drive over to Louisville with my two-man crew to pick up some equipment I had air freighted from California. I'll be back later in the afternoon. Will call then. I'm also at the Jefferson Hotel. Thanks, Richard Turner."

The other was from Graham Neal: "Welcome home, Bill. Give me a call when you get in. Can you and Ms. Luke join me, Marge, and Richard Turner and his two assistants for dinner at our house tomorrow night at seven-thirty? Neal."

After checking with Nancy, Bill called Neal and accepted the dinner invitation for both of them.

Once they were settled into their adjoining rooms on the third floor, Bill suggested they might want to take a walk around downtown Jefferson.

"Good idea. I need to stretch my legs after more than two hours in that cramped plane."

They walked out of the hotel and headed up Main Street toward the courthouse.

They had walked less than a block when Bill did a double take.

For several blocks, the north side of Main Street was lined with huge trucks. Traffic was blocked both ways on Main; city policemen and county sheriff's deputies were directing cars to side streets. Only the wide sidewalk on the south side of the street was open. Construction crews were working in the middle of the street, putting together what looked like a carnival. There was a partially assembled Ferris wheel and a merry-go-round complete with ponies and other animals. Parts of other rides were being unloaded from the trucks.

Suddenly, Bill felt a hand on his shoulder. He turned to face Dave Taylor.

"Hey, Dave. How are you?"

They shook hands and Bill introduced Dave to Nancy.

"Nancy Luke, this is Dave Taylor. He's the Sheriff of Madison County. We went to high school together. Nancy is my agent from New York."

"It's a pleasure to meet you Mr. Taylor. I've heard Bill speak of you."

"Likewise, ma'am. Well, Bill, guess you sure pulled it off. There's not a hotel vacancy anywhere around. Some people are having to get rooms in Louisville."

"What's all this about?"

"The movie people are building a carnival in the middle of Main Street for some of the scenes. At least that's what I was told. They're also starting to change the signs and some stuff on some buildings to make it look like Jefferson forty years ago. They're bringing in a bunch of old cars from that period. But they're not going to start filming for at least another two weeks. That's when Jack Turner and the actors arrive. Can you believe it? Brett Cooper in Jefferson! But the English-Frostmann people have already started hiring locals as extras. They set up an office at the old armory. I figured you'd show up then for the actual filming. How come you're here now?"

"Jack Turner's nephew, Richard Turner, is a documentary film maker and he's making a documentary about the filming of *Look Down*. He wanted to interview me and get that part out of the way before production gets into high gear."

"I guess that makes sense. Well, I got to get back to work. Give me a call when you get a chance, Bill. We need to talk. Nice to meet you, Ms. Luke."

Bill and Nancy turned south off Main Street and walked past the high school to the parkway along the riverfront.

"This really is a very pretty town, Bill."

"I always describe it as a town where Mark Twain could return and feel right at home." *Except for the shadows and secrets lurking just behind the carefully preserved nineteenth-century buildings. I wonder if Mark Twain ever saw a UFO? They were here then, just as they are now.*

Bill went on to explain to Nancy that the town's preservation efforts were partly out of civic pride and partly to attract bed-and-breakfast tourists looking for a calm weekend with a dose of nostalgia. Shopping malls and new housing developments were kept on the outskirts of town. The population had remained a stable eight thousand or so over the years, mainly because of Jefferson's relative isolation—which also saved its Neo-Classical and Federal architecture from developments spawned by growing populations. The town was just far enough away from Cincinnati, Louisville and Indianapolis so that it had never become a bedroom community for those cities. It existed on its own terms, supported mainly by farming, tourism, and some light manufacturing.

"I'm beginning to understand *Look Down* more. This must have been a wonderful place to grow up."

"It was." *Except for my best friend being repeatedly abducted by aliens from God-knows-where for God-knows-why.*

"Bill, what did the Sheriff mean when he said that 'you sure pulled it off'?"

"A lot of the locals here apparently think I had something to do with Turner picking Jefferson for the film. I wrote the book, and I grew up here, so I guess in a way they have a point.

But as you know, I had no direct influence over where Turner decided to shoot the film. I've given up trying to explain it."

"I'm thirsty. Where can a girl get a drink around here?"

"Let's walk back up to Main Street. There's a bar called the Oasis that's been there forever. It's now owned by a high school classmate named Jim Gassert. It's not fancy."

"Sounds good. Let's do it."

When they walked into the Oasis, Jim Gassert greeted them from behind the bar, which was three-quarters full. Two servers were waiting on customers in booths and at tables.

"Bill! Welcome. Come in."

Bill introduced Jim to Nancy.

Jim pointed across the narrow room.

"There's an empty booth. You want it or do you want to be at the bar?"

"The booth's fine," Bill replied.

When they were seated, Jim came from behind the bar to take their orders. Nancy wanted some water and a glass of white wine. Bill ordered beer.

Jim was beaming.

"I'm sure glad you got that movie company to come here. My business has quadrupled ... heck, more than quadrupled."

Nancy smiled at Bill.

When Jim brought their drinks, he looked at Bill.

"You still interested in UFOs?"

"Why?"

"Well, I thought about you recently. About a week ago one of those workmen for the movie company came in here just as I made the last call before closing. He looked like he'd seen a ghost. Said he had taken a late-night walk along the river-front and saw some kind of big machine just hanging in the air. Claimed it was silent and shaped like a triangle. He'd been drinking, so nobody in the bar, including me, paid much attention to him. Later, I remembered our conversation. Was it back in March?"

"Yeah. I was just curious about those sightings I had read about earlier in the Courier."

"Oh, right."

Jim quickly returned to the bar to wait on four people who had just come in.

Nancy gave Bill a puzzled look.

"UFOs? I didn't know you were a UFO buff. When did you get interested in them?"

"When I came out here last year to help Paul Watson find his daughter, I discovered there had been a number of UFO sightings in and around Jefferson. I admit I found it intriguing. Curiosity and my reporter's instincts, I guess. Then when I was here in March to meet Turner, Jim and I discussed the sightings. He said a few of his customers had also reported seeing strange things in the sky at night. But I imagine most of them had been drinking a bit. That's kind of all there is to it. *Here I am lying to Nancy. But I don't know what else to do right now. I think she'll understand when I tell her the full story. I hope so.*"

Bill's cell phone chimed.

"Hello."

"Bill, it's Richard Turner. I'm back from Louisville. Can we get together?"

"Sure. I'm with Nancy Luke, my agent. We're just down the street having a drink. We can be back at the hotel in fifteen minutes."

"Great. What time is it now?"

"A little after four."

"Okay. I'll meet you in the lobby."

When Bill tried to pay his and Nancy's tab, Jim refused to take his money.

"It's on the house. I owe you."

✳

If Jack Turner's rumpled look and droopy, Bassett-hound eyes hadn't fit Bill's image of a Hollywood type, his nephew more than made up for it.

Richard Turner was in his late thirties, well over six feet tall with straw-blond hair. He was wearing a khaki safari jacket, blue jeans, and tan desert boots. In a recent profile in The Los Angeles Times, he was described as looking like a taller version of a much-younger Robert Redford.

"You must be Richard Turner. I'm Bill Sanders. This is Nancy Luke, my agent."

"I've heard a lot about both of you from my uncle. All good, I might add. Ms. Luke, you've known him for a long time, right?"

"Please, call me Nancy. Yes, we go back a long way. Before I got married, he and I were an occasional 'item,' as they say."

"No kidding. He never told me that."

"It was a long time ago."

Richard turned to Bill.

"I suggest we sit here in the lobby and discuss our plans. Then later how about if the three of us, along with my cameraman and soundman—who are both taking naps at the moment—go to dinner somewhere. The town's getting crowded and it's getting late. Should we try to make a reservation? Any recommendations?"

"Well, there's a Chinese restaurant within walking distance that I've heard is pretty good. That sound okay?"

Both Nancy and Richard nodded.

Bill turned and walked over to the registration desk. He knew Steve, the desk clerk, from his earlier stay at the hotel in March.

"Steve, can you give me the name and number of that Chinese restaurant just a few blocks from here? I want to make a reservation for tonight."

"They don't take reservations there, Mr. Sanders. You just have to wait. But it's a big place and things move pretty quickly. Good food, by the way."

"That's what I hear. Thanks, Steve."

Bill turned back to Nancy and Richard.

"No reservations. But let's give it a shot anyway. Maybe about seven?"

"That would be fine for me," Nancy replied. "While you two guys talk down here, I'm going to my room and rest a bit.

That walk and the wine made me a little sleepy. Bill, will you knock on my door about fifteen minutes before you're ready to go?"

"Yes, of course."

Nancy headed to the elevator; Bill and Richard settled into a couple of club chairs in a quiet corner of the lobby.

"So, Richard, what's the plan? I'm at your disposal."

"Basically, I want to do a series of interviews with you about your growing up here and how you came to write *Look Down*. I don't want them to be scripted. I want to just let you talk. I want to have freewheeling, spontaneous discussions about your life and how it's reflected in the novel. How much is fiction? How much is fact? I want to do the interviews in places Turner has selected for shoots. The high school. The farm. The bridge over the creek where the rabbits were drowned."

"That never really happened."

"Save it for the interview."

"How long will all this take?"

"At least four or five days. Some of the interviews might have to be shot several times. By the way, I hope you don't mind a little makeup. I've hired a local beautician to be with us for the entire shoot. Basically, it's just a little powder so your face doesn't look shiny."

"I understand. I've had to do that when I've been on TV from time to time."

"Well, let's try to get started about eight in the morning. I've rented a van that will hold all of us and the equipment. Will Nancy be coming along?"

"I don't know, but I doubt it. We can ask her at dinner."

Bill was happy the wait for a table for five at the Chinese restaurant was only about twenty minutes. Their waiter said business had been booming since English-Frostmann came to town.

The group was a good mix, despite their age differences. Vince Hubbard, the cameraman, and Saul Merkel, the soundman, had been out of college only a year or so and were just beginning to get a foothold in Hollywood. Both had a good sense of humor and were obviously happy Richard had hired them for the *Look Down* documentary project. Richard was relaxed, and it was infectious. Nancy was more chatty than usual; Bill was curious about all things Hollywood, especially the language and customs.

After a round of beers and appetizers they all ordered different dishes, plus an extra, and agreed to share.

Bill asked Nancy if she was going to go with them tomorrow for the filming of the interviews.

"I would like to, but only for half the day. I'll drive our rental car so I can come back early. I brought my laptop, and I have work to do. Plus, we're all going to dinner at the Neal house at seven-thirty, right?"

Bill nodded.

"Yes, seven-thirty. Richard, have you talked to or met Graham Neal?"

"Nope. All I know about him is a note at the hotel inviting me, Vince, and Saul to dinner. His email was on the note. That's how we accepted."

"I know he knew you were coming, but how did he know about Vince and Saul?"

"I have no idea."

"Well, not much goes on in this town that he doesn't know about. You'll like him, I predict."

✳

The first day of interviewing was slower and more difficult than Bill expected. They were shooting outside a barn at a local farm that looked a bit like the Sanders family farm, long gobbled up by a subdivision. Scenes and sections of interviews had to be shot and reshot several times. Richard Turner was extremely professional and a perfectionist.

Describing his childhood in Indiana and his friendship with Paul Watson and his estrangement from his younger brother who was killed in a Texas prison brawl caused an occasional wave of melancholia to wash over Bill. *I can't talk about the most important thing in my past, which I only recently learned about from Paul's notebook. That I was somehow repeatedly paralyzed while my friend was abducted by aliens in UFOs. Will I ever be able to talk about that?*

Richard called it a day around four-thirty and the four of them headed back to the Jefferson Hotel to get ready for dinner. Nancy had left a little after noon.

Dinner at Neal's was enjoyed by all. Neal and his wife, Marge, lived in a riverfront mansion that had been built by his grandfather. Marge, who visited a cousin in London for several weeks every other year or so, had decorated the house, from slipcovers to china, with an English flair. Cocktails, including Neal's famous martinis, were served in the spacious living room.

Neal cooked thick steaks on an outdoor grill. Salad, baked potatoes, and several bottles of California Cabernet Sauvignon rounded out the main menu. Dessert was strawberry pie with whipped cream.

After dinner, the group adjourned to the living room for coffee and more conversation. Saul and Vince were full of questions for Neal about Jefferson and his years of running the Courier. Nancy and Marge had hit it off from the beginning and were discussing architecture and the history of the town. Bill and Richard discussed plans for the next few days of interviews.

It was eleven before the party broke up.

Marge and Nancy announced that they were going to be spending the next couple of days together touring some of Jefferson's historic homes.

Back at the hotel, Bill was just getting ready to climb into bed when his watch began to vibrate. The number four was on the face. Morgen!

Bill fished the phone Jake had given him out of his pants pocket.

"Hello. Morgen?"

"Bill. God, I miss you."

"I miss you, too."

"Where are you?"

"In Jefferson doing the interviews for that documentary Jack Turner's nephew is making about the filming of *Look Down*."

"When will you be back in New York?"

"Not for four or five more days. Nancy Luke is with me. We had dinner tonight at Graham Neal's house with Turner's nephew and two of his crew members."

"Have you heard anything from anyone else. Jake? Max?"

"No. But I didn't expect to. Max is working on the problem of those three Secret Service agents. That's not going to be easy."

"I know. But I may have some good news."

"What?"

"Remember Tom, the young guy up here who gave me the flight data and manifests for those two helicopters that landed at the New Mexico ranch with Duncan and Walker?"

"Sure. Didn't he get those from some computer whiz who works out there for The Seven? The guy mailed them to Tom's parents, right?"

"Yes. But listen to this. Both Tom and the computer whiz—his name is Jesse Copeland—have been comparing notes and have become increasingly disillusioned with The Seven and suspicious of what it is doing. Jesse has found a file on one of the computers in New Mexico that is locked down under several layers of security. The file is labeled The New Order and next to the title is the image of a coiled rattlesnake. The only reason Jesse is interested in it is because it's so secure. Tom says Jesse sees getting into the file without being detected as a challenge. But, Bill, that file could have something to do with

Snakebite. It could be the smoking gun we need to convince the President."

"Sounds possible. Do you think Jesse can access it and get it to us undetected?"

"I don't know, but I'm sure he's going to try based on what Tom said. Should we alert Jake and Max?"

"Not yet. We can't do anything now anyway until those three agents are out of the way. Let's wait until I get back to New York."

"I'm not sure I'll be able to come to New York as easily as the last two times."

"I understand. We need to be careful. Especially right now. I want you safe and in my arms. I love you, Morgen."

"I love you, too."

Bill went to sleep thinking of Morgen and wishing she was in bed beside him.

Bill was lost in a deep wood. It was dark and he was barely able to follow a faint path, probably made by animals.

Then, suddenly and without explanation, he was standing on the edge of a cliff, overlooking a vista that included a vast plain and a distant mountain range. There were dark clouds in the distance, but overhead the night sky was clear. There was no wind. All was silent. He could clearly see Orion and the Big Dipper.

Then, to his bewilderment, seven of the brightest stars from both constellations began to move about in the sky. They got brighter and moved closer until they formed a giant upside-down V above his head.

"Spectacular, isn't it?"

The sound of a voice in the quiet darkness startled Bill. He turned to see Colonel Richard West standing beside him, dressed in the same brown three-piece suit and green tie he had worn the first, and only, time they met last year.

"What is it?"

"It's one of the alien ships I told you about."

"What's it doing here? How do stars turn into a UFO? Why is it showing itself to me?"

"So many questions! You are a good reporter. But I don't know the answer to any of them. Nobody does. Remember our talk? Maybe

you're a key to all this. Then again, maybe not."

With that, West turned and walked away into the darkness.

Bill looked up to the sky. The seven V-shaped lights were gone. Orion and the Big Dipper looked as normal as ever.

Bill sat down and put his head on his knees.

When he looked up it was daylight. Off to his left was Morgen running toward him, calling his name. A phone started ringing.

Bill rolled over in bed and picked up the hotel phone on his bedside table. An automated voice told it was six in the morning. Richard Turner would be ready to go back to work at eight.

The following days of filming and interviews were tiring and tedious for Bill, mainly because he was distracted by thoughts of Morgen and The Seven. Nancy spent most of the time with Marge Neal. One day the two drove to Louisville to shop and have dinner.

Richard Turner finished the interviews late in the afternoon on the fourth day, Sunday. Back at the hotel, he thanked Bill and shook his hand.

"I hope this is what you wanted."

"It's perfect. Now I just have to film the actual making of the movie in a couple of weeks. Then splice your stuff in. But I'll probably go back to L.A. the day after tomorrow, depending on some random shots I want to get of Jefferson in the process of being transformed into itself forty years ago. I also need to stash our equipment until we need it in two weeks. Luckily, the hotel agreed to let us use its basement. When are you going back to New York?"

"Hoping for tomorrow. I have to call in the morning about the English-Frostmann plane. But they may not be able to pick me and Nancy up on such short notice. If that's the case, it'll be on Tuesday. Too bad we're not headed west so we could take you along."

"Thanks, but Saul, Vince, and I have reservations out of

Louisville. By the way, are you coming back when the filming starts?"

"I'm going to try. I'm anxious to meet Brett Cooper and Simon Carey."

"Simon's a good little kid. Very talented. But Brett's another story. He's tough to work with. Full of himself. He can be a real shit. I've known him for a long time. Turner is lukewarm about working with him but knows he's a good actor and a big box-office draw. They get along, but just barely."

❋

On Monday morning, Bill and Nancy shared a late breakfast at the hotel.

"I called about the plane. It can't be here until tomorrow at noon."

"That's fine with me. I've got a couple of hours of work to do, and then I think Marge and I will spend the afternoon together. There's a couple more houses she wanted to show me. She knows everyone and has an amazing knowledge of Jefferson."

"Sounds like you two really hit it off."

"We did. I've invited her to visit me in New York between Thanksgiving and Christmas."

"That's great. I was afraid you'd be bored here."

"Just the opposite. It's a fascinating little town. As I said earlier, you were lucky to have spent most of your childhood here."

"I know." *Except for the weird events that only revealed themselves in the last year.*

Bill glanced out the dining room window, which looked out on Main Street. He saw Dave Taylor drive by in a brown and tan police cruiser. *Damn, I forgot all about Dave. The first day we were here I promised to give him a call and get together for a talk.*

"You look distracted."

"I just remembered something I have to do today."

"Well, I'm off to my room and work. I'll probably be back

later in the afternoon. Let's plan on dinner somewhere tonight."

"How about the Oasis down the street? It's where we had a drink the first day we got here. It's just a bar, nothing elegant, but they sure have good hamburgers and fries."

"Perfect."

Nancy stood up, patted Bill on the shoulder, and headed toward the elevator.

Bill ordered another cup of coffee and reached for his cell phone.

"Madison County Sheriff's office."

"Is Dave Taylor in?"

"Who's calling?"

"Bill Sanders."

"Oh, Mr. Sanders. I think he just pulled up out front. Hold on."

The waiter brought Bill's coffee.

"Bill?"

"Hi, Dave. Sorry I didn't get back to you sooner, but Richard Turner kept me busy from morning until night for the last four days. I'll be leaving tomorrow, but I'm free the rest of today if you have time to get together."

"Sure. Good idea. Let's meet at the Jefferson Cafe at two. The lunch crowd will be gone by then and we can talk."

"Okay. See you then."

Bill finished his coffee and walked out to the hotel parking lot. He had decided to drive around a bit before meeting Dave.

He headed out of town toward Paul Watson's house.

When he pulled into the clearing in front of the two-story log cabin, he could see that it was still closed up and nobody had been living there. The grass was cut, but the exterior logs were beginning to look a little dirty and water stained. He wondered how long Sharon would keep the place.

He got out of the car just as a cloud passed in front of the sun, casting a shadow over the area. He felt a little shiver and the hairs on the back of his neck stood up. *I can't tell Dave or Sharon what I know. Not yet, anyway. Maybe soon if things work out.*

Sharon deserves to know the truth that will bring some closure for her, although the truth will also bring her the knowledge that Cindy is dead, and Paul was murdered. Dave will probably be very pissed at me if he learns the truth and knows that I didn't keep my part of our agreement to share information.

The cloud passed and the sun came out again. Bill immediately felt better. He looked at the sky above the roof of the cabin and thought of Paul's description of what he saw above the house the night Cindy disappeared. *A big goddamn machine shaped like a triangle, bigger than the house and the clearing, was just hanging there in the sky about a hundred feet over the roof. It was absolutely silent.*

Next, he drove to the spot where Paul had crashed his Jeep into a culvert. He parked the car on the side of the road and got out for a closer look. There were still streaks of the Jeep's red paint on the culvert and some of the concrete was cracked and chipped.

He heard the cough of an engine and looked to the east across a narrow field. There was Joshua Baker on his tractor just as he had been last year right after Paul was killed. Then, he had told Bill he had seen a low-flying black helicopter just before Paul crashed into the culvert. *It was all black and didn't have no markings. And the windows was all dark. Like them limousines you see on TV.* Bill passed Baker's account on to Dave Taylor, who dismissed it out of hand because of Baker's notoriously bad eyesight. Only later did Colonel West confirm that account to Bill.

Bill walked over to a fence and waved at Baker. Baker shut his tractor off and walked toward Bill.

"Can I help you?"

"Mr. Baker, I'm Bill Sanders. I talked to you last year right after Paul Watson was killed when he crashed into that culvert in his Jeep."

"Of course. My eyesight ain't the best, but my memory still works. You're back in town with them movie folks, I guess."

"That's right."

"I promised my wife we'd get into town when the filming starts."

"Mr. Baker, you told me last year that you saw a black helicopter flying low just before Paul's wreck. Did the Sheriff or anybody in authority ever question you about that?"

"Nope. You're the only person I ever talked to about it. I know my eyes are bad, but it's hard to miss a helicopter. Especially with all that noise."

"I guess it would be. Well, thanks for talking to me again. I've got to go back to New York tomorrow, but I may be back in a couple of weeks when the filming starts. Maybe I'll see you then."

"I hope so. So long now."

Bill stood by the fence and Josh Baker returned to his tractor. *A half-blind man saw what was going on and nobody would believe him.*

✳

Dave Taylor looked tired but was in a cheerful mood when he met Bill at the Jefferson Cafe. Both ordered coffee.

"You say Jack Turner's nephew's been keeping you busy?"

"Yes, but it's over now. I'm flying back to New York at noon tomorrow."

"From Jefferson Field?"

"Yes. The English-Frostmann jet again."

"Is your agent, Nancy ...?"

"Luke."

"Nancy Luke. Is she going back with you?"

"Yes."

"I heard from one of my deputies that you were out at the Watson place earlier today. He just happened to drive by while you were there."

"I just wanted to see the place one more time. It's looking a little shabby around the edges." *Not much goes unnoticed in a small town.*

"I know. I've been meaning to call Sharon and find out if she's decided anything about selling it. But I put it off after you told me how pissed she was at you over Paul's crazy UFO story. But I got to call her sometime, I guess."

"She's still in Indianapolis? She hasn't been back here since she left last year?"

"Far as I know. Still at her parents' house."

"Neal thinks she's keeping the house here in the hope that Cindy will return someday and have a familiar place to return to."

"Makes sense, I guess. But I think Cindy's dead."

"It's been a long time, no question." *She's dead all right. She died among strangers who had injected her with powerful drugs. Her ashes were dumped in a cold river in West Virginia.*

Bill stirred some more cream into his coffee.

"Dave, remember when I was here last year there were those stories in the Courier about people seeing UFOs? We wondered then if that wasn't what inspired Paul's account to me, you, and Sharon about Cindy's abduction."

"Yeah, I remember. Kids out later than they should be, smoking pot. And drunks. Why?"

"I just wondered if there had been any more reports since then."

"Not in the paper. Neal at some point decided not to print them anymore. But my office gets a call now and again, usually at night, from someone reporting something strange in the sky. Usually over the river. Most of the time it's still kids or drunks. Why do you ask?"

"Just curious, I guess. A reporter's habits are hard to break."

"By the way, are we still in agreement to tell each other whatever we know or find out about Cindy Watson?"

"Yes, of course."

"You got anything to tell me?"

"No, nothing." *If I told you what I know you would probably try to have me committed.*

"Neal was pushing me pretty hard, especially on the murder of Daniel Scott. But he's eased up some lately. This is the toughest case I've ever been involved in. We have absolutely nothing on the Scott murder. No leads. No nothing. And it's like Cindy Watson just disappeared into thin air. Nothing. Nothing. Nothing. The State Police and the FBI have pretty much thrown up their hands. Plus, a lot of stuff is on hold right now because of the movie and the crowds in town."

"It's only going to get worse. Wait until Brett Cooper shows up in a couple of weeks."

"Lord, help us. But we sure like the business."

CHAPTER 13

Bill and Nancy got into Teterboro just in time to hit the rush hour traffic. Luckily, the driver they had arranged to have meet them was experienced and knew all the shortcuts and how to avoid problem areas. Nevertheless, by the time Bill dropped Nancy off at her apartment on Park Avenue, it was pushing six when he finally got to Eastside Towers.

George Carson was on duty.

"Good evening, Mr. Sanders. Welcome home."

"Thanks, George. It's good to be back."

As soon as Bill was inside his apartment, he pulled out the special phone Jake had given him and punch three for Max. No answer. *Must be in a meeting or talking to somebody. He'll call back.*

Bill unpacked his suitcase and was about to see what was in the refrigerator that he could have for dinner when his watch started vibrating. The number three appeared on the face.

"Hello, Max."

"Are you back in New York?"

"Yes, I just got in."

"Have you talked to the others?"

"Only Morgen. And that was a few days ago. She may be onto something that can help us, but I want her to explain it to the group. Can we have a conference call later tonight?"

"Yes. How about midnight eastern time. Can you call Morgen and Jake and alert them?"

"Yes. One more thing. Any progress on those three Secret Service guys?"

"I think so, but I won't know for sure until tomorrow. I'll explain at midnight. The four of us may be able to meet with the President, Ben Watkins, and Colonel Favate sooner than we think."

"Morgen may not be able to make the meeting. She's worried about trying to leave Maine again."

"Is she in any danger?"

"I don't think so. I hope not. She just doesn't want to make them suspicious."

"I understand. Talk to you later."

"Okay. Bye."

First, Bill called Jake.

"Midnight eastern time? That's only nine here. I guess I can stay up that late."

"Morgen has some interesting news for us, and I think Max is going to report progress on the Secret Service. We'll all get on the same page when we talk."

Bill called Morgen next.

"Bill, I'm a little worried about talking from my apartment. It could be bugged. Right now, I'm at a pharmacy. I think at midnight I'll go out to my car. I can still get the WiFi signal there pretty well."

"That might be a good idea."

"Bill, I have some news that makes me nervous."

"What is it?"

"The Seven wants me to go out to the ranch in New Mexico in about two weeks. They haven't said for how long. Bill, that compound is in the middle of ten thousand acres. The Seven control all the ways in and out."

"Why do they want you to go there?"

"I'm not sure. Something about helping with some data they need crunching. The upside is that it would put me close to Jesse Copeland, the computer whiz."

"I don't like it. Morgen, I can't stand the thought of you being in any danger. Or in more danger. Let's discuss it later with the others. Does this mean if we get cleared for a meeting with Stanton, you won't be able to attend?"

"Probably."

✳

The midnight conference call took about thirty minutes.

First, Morgen told the others about the computer file in New Mexico that Jesse Copeland was trying to access.

Jake was the first to react.

"It's called The New Order and has the image of a rattlesnake next to the title? We've got to see that. What are this kid's chances of cracking it?"

"I don't know. My friend in Maine, Tom—his last name is Norris—says Jesse is among the best when it comes to computers. A natural, Tom says."

"Well, let's hope so."

Morgen then disclosed that The Seven was sending her to New Mexico. She repeated what she had told Bill: She was concerned because access in and out of the New Mexico compound was totally controlled by The Seven.

"Access to the New York compound is not as tightly controlled, which makes me think that more important stuff is going on in New Mexico. That might explain why The New Order computer file is there. But, again, we don't know it's not on a computer in Ulster County. I guess it doesn't matter. If we can get it, it's not important where it came from."

Max spoke up.

"Morgen, do you think you're in any danger? You said they had quit paying much attention to you."

"I just don't know."

Jake interrupted.

"I don't think they would send you out here if they didn't trust you. If the New Mexico ranch is their main operations center, why would they send someone there they were suspicious of?"

"You may be right. I hope so."

Bill broke in.

"I take your point, Jake, but I still don't like it. We have to protect Morgen. Did you tell me earlier that they wanted you to go in two weeks, Morgen?"

"Yes. They said maybe in a couple of weeks. I need to tie up some details on the Maine project."

There was a pause of a few seconds. Then Max coughed and started to talk.

"Two weeks might give us time to make some kind of move. Listen, the problem of the three Secret Service agents may be resolved sooner than we thought. I'll know tomorrow. Turns out one of those agents has been under internal investigation for cheating on his expense account. He'll be offered the opportunity to resign quietly or face charges. Ben is promoting the second agent into his office with a fat raise. The third is being assigned to the Vice President's detail because an agent there had to take sick leave. None of this is a done deal yet, but it's very close. We may be able to have our meeting with the President as early as next week. Probably at Camp David."

Morgen interrupted.

"I don't think I'll be able to make it. I made two trips to New York without any problems. I think a third trip so soon might be pushing my luck. Especially since I should be getting ready to go to New Mexico."

"Well, let's see how things move in the next day or two. Then let's have another midnight conference call. The President is ready as soon as the three agents are out of the picture. In fact, he seems almost anxious. Sometimes I think it's as if he knows something we don't. Strange."

Max Burris orchestrated another midnight conference call two days later, on Thursday.

"Okay, guys, this is it. The two Secret Service transfers are complete, and I don't think they aroused any suspicion. Stanton is ready to meet with us. Both Cole Favate and I are super-sensitive about security, as is the President. The White

House is just too public and constantly being watched by the press. Stanton wants us to meet at Camp David Saturday afternoon at four. We'll gather at Aspen Lodge, where the President normally stays. But we'll hold our meeting in the bunker under Aspen Lodge. But it's more than a bunker. It's a bomb shelter, a war room, and a command center. It's huge, and it's electronically impenetrable. Absolutely bug-proof. The President can do anything from Camp David that he could do from the White House, the Pentagon, or Air Force One. He, Ben Watkins, and I will fly there late Friday afternoon on Marine One. Just the three of us and a small Secret Service detail and the military aide who follows the President with the so-called Football, the case containing the nuclear launch codes. No other aides or secretaries. There will only be a skeletal staff at Camp David. Favate will drive up that night. We want to stagger our arrivals, so we hopefully stay under the radar. Bill, can you come to D.C. tomorrow and then drive up Saturday morning, so you arrive at about eleven?"

"Yes, no problem. I'll be at the Hay-Adams. If I can't get reservations there, I'll let you know where I'm staying Friday night."

"Jake, can you also fly out here tomorrow and drive up so that you arrive at about two on Saturday?"

"No problem. Even if I have to charter a plane. I'll be at the Mayflower unless you hear otherwise."

"Good. The drive up to Camp David from D.C. takes about an hour and a half. The guards at the main gate will be alerted and will escort you to Aspen Lodge. Just show them some ID. Morgen, I'm assuming you aren't going to be able to make it, right?"

"Right. I'm afraid not."

"Don't worry. We'll keep you informed. Oh, I almost forget. President Stanton wants us to have dinner with him in Aspen Lodge Saturday night. He also wants us all to spend the night. There are several lodges, or cabins, and plenty of room. We can leave at various times on Sunday."

✳

When the conference call was finished, Bill called Jake.

"You want to have dinner tomorrow night in D.C.?"

"Good idea. Where? When?"

"How about the restaurant in my hotel where we had that great rack of lamb. It's called The Lafayette. Is seven a good time for you?"

"Perfect. See you then."

When his call with Jake ended, Bill then pressed four on the special iPhone. No answer. Two minutes later his watch vibrated.

"Bill, I'm glad you called. If you hadn't, I was going to call you."

"Are you okay? Are you in your car?"

"Yes, but I'm apprehensive. These people don't fool around."

"I know. Listen, Morgen, is there some way you could just leave? Come here and stay with me?"

"No. They would find me. I'll just have to go along with them and see what happens."

"I guess. But I worry about you. I love you."

"I worry about me, too. And I love you, too."

"We'll talk after the meeting with Stanton. Maybe something will change. I don't know."

"I understand. Sleep well. I wish I could be there beside you."

"You will soon. Remember that."

Morgen stifled a sob, said goodbye and ended the call.

It was after two when Bill finally went to sleep.

When Bill arrived at the Hay-Adams restaurant Friday evening, Jake was already seated at a table. He was wearing a dark blue suit with a red tie and sipping a large martini.

Jake stood up when he saw Bill walking toward the table. They shook hands.

As soon as Bill was seated, a waiter approached and asked

if he wanted a drink.

"I'll have what he's having."

"Very good, Sir."

Jake took a sip of his drink.

"Bill, you look worried. Something the matter?"

"I'm worried about Morgen. I think she's in a dangerous spot, even without being sent to New Mexico."

"I don't know. I still think The Seven sending her there is a sign of trust."

"Maybe. But I'm concerned about her being trapped on that access-controlled ranch if something goes wrong or if there's some sort of police or military action."

"I take your point. Look, Bill, why don't you discuss this with Stanton after we brief him at the meeting. Maybe you could pull him aside and discuss Morgen's situation with him before or after dinner. I assume you're going to stay for dinner and spend the night."

"Well, yes. But the President?"

"How many people get to have dinner with the President? Take advantage of it. He may have some good advice or be able to help in some way. I've never met him, but I'm told he's a decent guy. And the two of you have something in common: You both recently lost your wives. You're getting to Camp David at eleven, right?"

"That's right."

"I'm not arriving until two. That should give you a chance to get to know him a bit. Surely there'll be a lunch of some kind. Once you're comfortable with him, ask if you can meet with him privately after we have our group meeting in the bunker or whatever it's called. By the way, I'm bringing three more of our super iPhones, one for the President, one for Ben Watkins, and one for Cole Favate. That way we can all stay in touch without alerting anyone. I told Max. He thought it was a good idea."

"You better wait until after our meeting to hand them out. That way they'll fully understand."

"Good point."

The waiter arrived with Bill's martini. He and Jake ordered salads and broiled sea bass with wild rice and vegetables.

Jake again urged Bill to talk to President Stanton about Morgen.

"Hell, Bill, you've dealt with Presidents before. You know how to talk to anybody."

"Well, I'll give it a shot. But I'm not sure what he could say or do."

"Don't underestimate the power of a President. Especially one who is as smart as Stanton. That's how my sources describe him: smart as hell. He's also really popular, which enhances his power and authority."

The waiter brought their salads. They ate them mostly in silence. After the main course, they both declined dessert but ordered coffee.

As Bill stirred cream into his coffee, he glanced at Jake.

"It would be great if that computer file in New Mexico gave us a look at what Snakebite really is, what it plans. I still have a hard time believing that a group like The Seven—hell, any group—would have the power to overthrow the government, despite Colonel West's letter."

"Bill, remember what I said when we met at your apartment. Democracies are fragile. Especially old ones like ours. It depends on everybody following the rules and customs. But over the decades we've allowed power to shift to the top. And we've allowed this power to be concentrated in the executive branch. Forget that civics crap you learned in school about the three equal parts of the government. One, the executive, is more equal than the other two. Remember learning that only Congress can declare war? You know when that last happened? When the Japanese attacked Pearl Harbor in 1941. All the wars since then have come at the behest of the President. Congress either gave some meaningless legislative nod or looked the other way. Those craven bastards turned one of their most vital constitutional responsibilities over to the executive branch."

Jake paused before continuing.

"If The Seven makes its move against the President and a handful of other movers and shakers here, they just might pull it off. Especially if the coup was coupled with some catastrophic event like 9/11. My experience and my gut tell me that's what they're planning. The President and the country are in grave danger. We have to convince him."

"I agree. But I've also been thinking that we're ignoring the elephant in the room: the reality of UFOs and aliens. That is, if we believe Colonel West and those pictures Warren Holden hid in the doghouse are real, which I believe they are. Warren wouldn't have had them if they weren't."

"Yes, but what else can we do? The aliens ignore us completely. They only react to us when they think we threaten them. They apparently have been here for thousands of years. We don't have a clue what they're up to. But we do know what The Seven is up to. We can't deal with UFOs and the aliens. But we just might be able to deal with The Seven. Or what The Seven has become."

CHAPTER 14

Bill pulled up to the entrance of Camp David about five minutes before eleven. After the uniformed guards checked his ID and patted him down, they told him to park his rental car in a small, paved area next to the entrance. One of the guards pointed to a golf cart.

"Here's your ride to Aspen Lodge. Hop in." The guard put Bill's small overnight bag on the floor of the golf cart in front of the rear seat.

In a couple of minutes Bill was dropped off at the front door of Aspen Lodge, where Max was waiting for him.

"Welcome to Camp David. Listen, Bill. I wanted to talk to you privately for a minute. We're really having this meeting for three people: President Stanton, Ben Watkins, and Colonel Favate. When we meet at four, I'm going to propose that you start things off by telling your story, from your friend's phone call for help to the present, for those three. In addition, I want you to explain the pictures. I guess I'm asking if that's okay. I didn't want to pull any surprises on you."

"That's fine, Max. It all has to come out one way or the other."

"Good. Come on in and meet the President."

President Stanton was sitting in a large club chair near a fireplace. The interior of the lodge was as warm and rustic as the outside indicated.

Stanton stood up and warmly shook hands with Bill.

"Hello, Mr. Sanders. It's a pleasure. May I call you Bill?"

"Please do, Sir."

"I don't think we've met before. I have a pretty good memory for names and faces. I was looking at your bio last night, and it looks like you had the good sense to get out of Washington before I arrived."

"I'm not sure how much good sense was involved, but, yes, I left the Times more than ten years ago to write books."

"Well, I'm glad you did. I feel like I know you through *Points South*. I made it required reading at the State Department."

"Thank you, Mr. President."

"Now you've got a best-selling novel that is about to be made into a movie?"

"Yes. Jack Turner's the director and he's about to start shooting it on location in Indiana."

"Who are the actors?"

"It hasn't been announced yet, but Brett Cooper and Simon Carey."

"Oh, I know Cooper. He gave money to my last campaign and appeared with me at a couple of political rallies in California. He's a good actor, but he can be difficult."

"As I understand."

"Heck, who can't be at times. I also understand that you're hard at work on a new book about the Middle East that will be patterned after *Points South*."

"Yes, Sir. I'm finished with the reporting and have just starting writing. It should be finished in about eighteen months."

The President glanced at Max.

"Max, you've been awfully quiet."

"Just letting you two get to know each other a bit."

"We've got one more person to arrive, right? Jake McCoy, the ex-CIA agent. I understand he worked for a time in the Carter White House and became close friends with Walter Jansen. That was a shame about him being killed by a hit-and-run driver. He was a good man."

Bill and Max exchanged glances.

The President turned to Max.

"Where are Cole and Ben?"

"They went down to the bunker to check on some details. They should be here any minute."

Max had no sooner finished speaking when the sound of an elevator door opening could be heard coming from a nearby hallway.

"Here they are now."

Ben Watkins and Cole Favate walked into the main room. Favate was dressed in casual civilian clothes. Watkins, tall and imposing, was wearing a dark blue blazer and an open-collar dress shirt.

The President introduced them to Bill.

"You know what Ben does. He's too important to me and my administration not to be included in this group. Plus, we need him. Cole has been my closest friend since our childhood together in Ohio. He is now an Air Force colonel working for the Defense Intelligence Agency at the Pentagon. He knows the military inside out. I would trust him with my life. But there's another reason I wanted him included, which you'll understand later."

Max looked puzzled by Stanton's comment, but said nothing.

Both Watkins and Favate smiled as they shook Bill's hand. Watkins spoke first.

"It's a real pleasure to meet you, Mr. Sanders."

"Please call me Bill,"

"At the urging of my wife, I just finished reading *Look Down*. I'm anxious to see the movie. I read *Points South* a couple of years ago. Best thing I have ever read on that part of the world."

"Thank you. I appreciate that."

Favate, whose thick black hair and heavy eyebrows gave him a mildly sinister look, cleared his throat before speaking.

"I haven't read your novel, but I sure enjoyed *Points South*. I don't know anybody in my working group who hasn't read it."

"That's nice to hear. You're both very kind."

There was a short pause in the conversation. Then the

President asked about Morgen.

"I understand Morgen Remley won't be able to make it. Why not?"

Max answered.

"Sir, you'll understand fully when we meet later in the afternoon. It's complicated, and you need some background information, which we will provide. But let's wait until the meeting and we're all here."

"Okay, Max. You're the boss on this."

The President turned and headed toward the dining room.

"How about some lunch?"

✳

After White House stewards had cleared the table and everyone was finished with coffee, the President looked at his watch.

"We've got about forty-five minutes until Jake McCoy arrives. How about a little walk? It's a beautiful day. And later we're going to be stuck in that underground bunker."

"Good idea, Sir," Max said.

The President led the group out the front door of Aspen Lodge. As soon as he was outside, four Secret Service agents took up positions around him and the group but at a discreet distance.

The group followed Stanton down some stone steps and around the edge of a large swimming pool.

Stanton pointed to the figure-eight-shaped pool.

"Nixon had this pool built. He wanted it in just this spot. The engineers told him that it would be over the underground bunker, which wasn't strong enough to support the pool's weight. They wanted to build it just a few feet farther away from the lodge. They explained that to build it where he wanted it would mean reinforcing the bunker at an extra cost of about a quarter-million dollars. Nixon insisted they do it. That pool wound up costing more than a half-million dollars. Twice as much as it was supposed to. And that was in nineteen-seventy dollars. I think Nixon took the extra money from some Pentagon slush fund."

They walked on, following Stanton down a path that took them away from Aspen Lodge. They stopped on a slight rise that gave them a visual sense of the entire two-hundred acres of Camp David.

The President clearly enjoyed the place.

Bill remembered the time he had spent covering the White House. The first time he was admitted into the West Wing, he was amazed at how small and cramped it was. And how much of a fishbowl it was. No wonder presidents like to come to Camp David.

Stanton started talking again.

"You know, when Jimmy Carter was elected, one of the first things he wanted to do was sell Camp David. He thought it was too expensive. His staff finally talked him out of it. Kind of ironic considering the role the place played in his administration and his place in history. There are ten or twelve separate lodges for guests. Each of you is assigned to one. A White House steward will take you to them after dinner."

One of the four Secret Service agents suddenly walked toward the group, pulled Ben Watkins aside, and whispered in his ear.

The President looked toward Ben.

"Excuse me, Sir, but I have to go to the gate. There's some sort of problem with Jake McCoy and some cell phones he's carrying in a bag.

The President nodded but looked puzzled.

Bill and Max glanced at each other and smiled.

As Watkins climbed into a golf cart, President Stanton waved his hand.

"Ben, we'll walk around a few minutes more and then meet you and Mr. McCoy back at the lodge."

"Very good, Sir."

About 10 minutes later, Max's watch began to vibrate and display the number two. Jake. Max pulled his phone out of his pocket.

"Jake?"

"No, it's Ben Watkins. I'm just checking out this phone to make sure it's actually a phone. Although it's a bit unusual. Mr. McCoy says this is his phone. But he has three others and three Apple watches."

"Ben, I should have mentioned this to you earlier. Those phones are okay. Same for the watches. They are for the President and you and Cole Favate. You'll understand after our meeting."

"Okay. Mr. McCoy and I will see you at the lodge in a few minutes."

✳

By the time the group had gathered at Aspen Lodge, it was nearly three o'clock. Max introduced Jake to the President, Ben Watkins, and Cole Favate.

The President put his hand on Max's shoulder.

"Max, is there any reason we can't go ahead and meet now instead of waiting until four?"

"No, Sir. The only reason we picked four was to give some leeway in case someone was late or delayed."

"Then let's do it."

The President walked over to a desk, opened a drawer, and pulled out a thin leather briefcase.

The six of them and two Secret Service agents took the elevator to the bunker under Aspen Lodge. The other two Secret Service agents stayed on the main floor of the lodge, guarding the entrance to the elevator.

When he stepped out of the elevator, Bill had a queasy feeling. The bunker looked too much like the one in New York where he had met Colonel West and lost Morgen. *We're also underneath a big swimming pool. I sure hope Nixon's engineers knew what they were doing.*

The President, still clasping the leather briefcase, led the way down a carpeted hallway to a big, well-lighted conference room. Ten high-back leather chairs surrounded a rectangular, highly polished wooden conference table. There were six bottles of water on the table in front of six of the chairs. Next to each water bottle was a thick file Max had place there earlier in the day. Each file was sealed with paper tape. The chair at the head of the table was taller than the rest and had the Presidential seal embossed on its back.

Max closed the heavy soundproof door as everyone took seats. The President carefully placed his leather case on the floor next to his chair. The two Secret Service agents who had accompanied them had taken positions outside the door, along with the military aide with the nuclear codes.

The President took a sip of water and looked around the table.

"I don't think I need to say this, but I'm going to anyway. We must all reaffirm our commitment to total secrecy within this group. I mean total. No notes. No recordings. Morgen Remley can be briefed, but I think Bill Sanders can handle that in a way that won't violate this mandate. I haven't requested that any of you be searched prior to this meeting, although you all probably have cell phones with voice recording apps. Make sure they're turned off. I don't have one with me. The glitch with Jake McCoy and his extra phones at the gate was cleared up and will be explained later. Right, Ben?"

"Yes, Sir."

Everyone at the table except the President pulled out a cell phone and made sure it was turned off.

"Well, it's crunch time. I've been patient about all this and agreed with Max's request that I hold off until we got together under great secrecy and he, Bill Sanders, and Jake McCoy could show me evidence of danger to the country and my presidency. Well, here we are. Show me."

Max spoke first.

"Please, everyone, do not open the files in front of you until I ask you to. You'll understand why in a short time. Mr. President, I think the best way for the three of us to convey to you what we know and what we think we know is to start at the beginning. The most direct way to do that is to let Bill

Sanders tell you of his experiences during the past year or so. From the beginning. I'm sorry Morgen Remley can't be here. She's an important part of the story. But her absence may end up helping us. We should know soon. Bill?"

"Mr. President, a year ago this spring I received a frantic telephone call for help from an old friend in Jefferson, Indiana. He said he needed help and that I was the only person ...."

For the next hour, Bill held the President and the others spellbound as he recounted all that had happened to him since that fateful phone call for help from Paul Watson that eventually led to his meeting with Colonel West. He made it clear that UFOs and aliens were a reality and had been present on Earth for thousands of years, maybe longer. He discussed the history of The Seven and how it had become powerful and morphed into a threat over the years. He explained his wife's death in a plane blown up by The Seven to stop an inquisitive congressman. He left nothing out except the fact that he had spent a night in the bed of Warren Holden's widow, Betty, in Santa Fe. It had not been a sexual encounter. Her husband had been dead for almost a year and she simply wanted someone to hold her and be close to her for the night. Bill felt it was personal and had no bearing whatsoever on the events he was recalling. He was open about his relationship with Morgen.

The President was ashen by the time Bill described the murder of Walter Jansen and the execution-style killing of Larry Sullivan by The Seven.

As Bill neared the end of his recounting, he described how Morgen had been able to get helicopter manifests and data that showed that Ross Duncan, the Senate majority leader, and Robert Duncan, the director of the CIA, had been at The Seven's New Mexico compound when they were supposed to be together on a fishing trip.

"We think they may be the two top leaders of The Seven. We're not sure which one is the chairman of the board, so to speak."

Bill also told the group about the computer file in New

Mexico labeled The New Order with the image of a coiled rattlesnake.

"We think that file may contain the plans for Operation
Snakebite. Morgen is working on getting a copy of it. As some
of you already know, she's being sent to the New Mexico ranch
in two weeks. There's a young computer whiz working for
The Seven at the ranch compound who has soured on the
group. We think he'll help Morgen get a copy of the file. But
it's dangerous. These are vicious people."

The President ran his fingers through his hair and looked
up at the ceiling.

"Jesus, this is unbelievable. But I believe it. Duncan and
Walker, for God's sake. Bob Walker and I were roommates in
college. But that explains something I've noticed about both
of them lately. Now I know what the list means that Jim Winston left for me. Max, have you shown that to the others?"

"It's in the file. They'll see it in a few minutes."

"Poor Jim. Why didn't he just come and talk to me. Why
did he have to kill himself?"

Jake McCoy spoke for the first time since the group had
entered the room.

"Maybe he was in too deep. Maybe he felt overwhelming
guilt for betraying you, Sir. It could have been something else
we have no knowledge of."

"Maybe so."

There was a long pause. The President appeared lost in
thought.

Max broke the silence.

"Now let's open the files in front of each of us."

The acoustics in the room amplified the sound of six pieces
of paper tape being torn at the same time.

Max held a copy of the top paper in each file. It was the
list Jim Winston had left for the President.

"Until a few seconds ago, I was the only person other than
President Stanton who had seen this. It was what caused me
to urge the President to meet with this group in the utmost
secrecy. Now we all know the meaning of this list. Clearly, Jim

was trying to warn the President but in a somewhat cryptic way."

Next was the copy of the letter Colonel West had sent to Bill from beyond the grave.

"Mr. President, Ben, and Cole. You three need to read this letter carefully. Right now."

The President nodded and pulled a pair of reading glasses from his shirt pocket.

There was silence in the room as the three men read.

When they were finished, Ben Watkins was the first to speak.

"This is incredible. I never heard of this Colonel West. Does anyone besides Bill know him?"

Cole Favate raised his hand.

"I don't know him. But I have seen his name on documents when he was stationed in Brussels with NATO. He's for real, if that's what you're asking."

Bill glanced at Colonel Favate.

"Well, if Morgen were here, she could vouch for West's reality and much of what he wrote in that letter."

The President seemed impatient.

"Go on, Max. What's next?"

Max picked up the lists Bill had found in Warren Holden's attic and the summaries that he and Jake had discovered in the doghouse Holden built with a hidden compartment.

"I'd like Jake to explain these."

"There's not a lot to explain, Max. Holden compiled several lists of people he believed were involved with The Seven. They were by no means complete but did contain the names of Duncan and Walker and Jim Winston, as well as the editor at the Post who was killed. The summaries explain the involvement of the names on the lists with The Seven. When they were recruited. What their roles are. What their day jobs are. That's how we learned that Duncan and Walker make up the top leadership. When Bill and I went on our road trip and mailed copies of these lists and summaries to everyone on them, we also included some photographs. You'll see them shortly. Maybe receiving this stuff in the mail is what pushed Jim Winston over the edge. I hope not. Suicide is psychologically very complex and seldom triggered by a single event. Or so I've read."

The President stood up, stretched, and took a long drink of water.

"What's next, Max?"

"Pictures, Sir. Bill will explain."

Bill picked up the first of four pictures, the black and white shot of the Lunar Lander taken from a good distance away. Hanging in the airless sky several hundred feet above the landing craft was a mammoth black, triangular-shaped craft. It was tilted up in the front, so the lights under the ship at the end of each of the triangles were visible. Its size was mind-boggling. Each of the three sides was hundreds of feet long.

"This picture was taken in July, 1969, when we first landed on the moon."

The President exhaled through clenched teeth.

"Who took it?"

"Well, Sir, it had to be either Neil Armstrong or Buzz Aldrin."

Ben Watkins spoke up.

"I've heard rumors that our astronauts had encountered UFOs, but I never took them seriously. How come Armstrong or Aldrin didn't report this?"

"Maybe they did," Bill replied. "But remember how The Seven works. Fear. Intimidation. Ridicule. Murder. Aldrin made some odd references to UFOs, for which he was ridiculed and marginalized. We think Warren Holden got these photos from somebody at NASA."

Bill then turned to the final three pictures, which were in color.

The first was a high-resolution close-up of the "face" on Mars that had graced the covers of newspapers and magazines around the world when it was released in 1976 by NASA.

"There's only one problem with this photograph. If you

look on the back, you'll see that it was taken two years ago by a secret mission to photograph the surface of Mars."

Ben Watkins interrupted.

"Why is that a problem, Bill?"

"Since the picture was released in 1976, NASA always dismissed the mile-wide face as a trick of light and shadows. That was supposedly proved in 1998 when the Mars Global Surveyor took more pictures of the face, and NASA released them to the public. All they showed was a flattened pile of rubble with a vague suggestion of a mouth and eyes. Light and shadows, NASA repeated. The mainstream media lost interest. But if what NASA said in 1998 was true, how could this picture have been taken two years ago? The obvious answer is that the 1998 photo was a fake, and this photo taken two years ago is the real thing."

Watkins looked a bit confused but nodded in agreement. The President had a subtle, slightly odd smile on his usually serious-looking face.

Bill continued.

"Now let's look at the third photograph."

It was also of the face. But sitting on the Mars surface in front of the face was a singular, black triangular craft that looked very much like the one floating above the Lunar Lander in the first picture.

"If the face is a mile wide, Jake and I have calculated that each side of that craft is a quarter of a mile long."

Bill then held up the fourth and final photo. It was a wider view of the face and the flat plain in front of it. Where the single black triangular object had been in the third photo, there were now eight such objects. They were arranged in a circular formation, looking like a pie whose slices were slightly separated.

"If you look on the backs, you'll see that these two pictures were taken two years ago by the same secret mission that took the second photo. Now I think you can see why earlier I talked about the reality of UFOs. You can also understand why I think Colonel West was truthful in his letter to me that was delivered more than six months after he died."

President Stanton put the four pictures side by side on the table in front of him. His earlier smile was gone.

"A mission to Mars, and the President knew nothing of it? Who authorized this? Where did the money come from?"

Max raised both hands in the air in a gesture of frustration.

"It had to be The Seven. Remember what West said, Sir. They have money from black budgets in the U.S. and all over the world. But why would they want a secret mission to Mars?"

Bill looked at Jake before responding.

"Remember what West said? The Seven is trying to cover up what the government doesn't know, but it's also trying to discover—without success, according to West—whatever the aliens are up to with their abductions, cattle mutilations, crop circles, and God knows what else. Maybe this was part of that effort. According to West, the aliens react to us only if they feel threatened. Obviously, they're not bothered by flybys and photographs. But those two goals of secrecy and discovery were why The Seven was created by Truman and are fairly benign compared with its evolved goal of insurrection. That's why we're here."

The President stood up. The other five reflexively started to stand until the President motioned for them to remain seated.

"When I showed Max that cryptic list that Jim Winston left for me, I had no idea of its meaning or importance. But it was clear that Max did. He didn't want to tell me anything then because he said he didn't have the proof that would back him up. He wanted me to meet with him, Bill, Jake, and Morgen. He insisted I pull Ben into this group, once we got rid of the three Secret Service agents who were part of The Seven. I insisted that Cole Favate, my closest friend since childhood, be included. That's because Cole is the reason that I didn't throw Max out of the Oval Office when he hinted of a threat to the country and to my presidency. I'll explain by showing you something."

The Present sat back down in his chair and reached for the leather case he had put on the floor next to the chair when he came into the room.

He pulled three nine-inch by twelve-inch manila envelopes out of the case. They were labeled No. 1, No. 2 and No. 3. The envelopes contained a total of eight pictures, which the president started passing one by one to the group.

"Sorry I don't have copies of these."

There was silence as the five passed the pictures around to each other.

Max was the first to speak.

"Holy shit! Excuse me, Sir."

"That's okay, Max. That was close to my reaction when I first saw them."

The pictures were of the same subjects as the ones Bill had explained earlier. Two appeared to be duplicates. Two had higher resolution and were much clearer. The face on Mars. The triangular craft. The dates matched the first set of photos that had been in the files with the other material.

A frown crossed the President's face.

"I don't understand why eight of the craft are gathered in a circle in front of the face. What's their connection to the face?"

Bill responded.

"Who knows? Jake and I have speculated that the face could be thousands of years old. Older than the pyramids on Earth. Maybe the aliens built it as a tribute to some thing or someone. Maybe it has some religious significance. Or maybe it marks the entrance to an underground facility. Remember, West said the aliens have bases on the moon and Mars."

Jake looked up over his reading glasses.

"Mr. President, where did you get these?"

"From Cole, a little over a year ago. We'd have to check dates, but I think it was around the same time Bill drove out to Indiana to help his friend find his missing daughter. Cole and I never looked at them together. He simply gave them to me and told me to look at them and destroy them. Obviously,

I didn't destroy them."

Max looked at Cole.

"Where did you get them, Cole?"

"From an old friend at NASA. I think he give them to be because he knew I was friends with President Stanton, and he wanted the President to see them."

"Was he involved with The Seven?"

"I don't think so. His name wasn't on Holden's lists."

The President sighed as he collected his eight photos and put them back in the leather case. He looked around the table.

"Now you know why I wanted Cole in this group. So, where the hell are we? We've got a couple of big problems on our hands. First, the UFOs and aliens. This is huge. For the future of the human race. For our history. It changes everything. I don't think anybody in this room doubts that there's been a massive cover-up of their existence since the end of the Second World War. There's also been an even bigger cover-up of the fact that the U.S. government doesn't have a clue about where they're from or what they're doing here. That has been coupled with a disinformation campaign to convince the public that the government knows what's going on and is keeping it secret for whatever reasons. The truth has to come out. Will it be as disruptive as Colonel West told Bill Sanders when they first met? Or will it be less disruptive than the threat posed by The Seven, as West wrote in his letter to Bill? Did West change his mind between the meeting with Bill and the letter? Or had he already changed his mind by the time of the meeting and was just giving Bill the party line? I'm of the opinion that we must come clean with the public on this, despite whatever problems it might cause. The question is how and when. We need to work out a plan for that.

"Our second problem is The Seven and what they're up to. Are they planning a coup? Was West right? When are they going to attempt it and how? Hopefully that computer file in New Mexico will tell us. Right now, our only hope of getting it lies with Morgen Remley and a young man in New Mexico. Do we even know his name?"

"Yes. Jesse Copeland," Bill replied.

The President continued.

"We've got to get our hands on that New Order file before it's too late. Anybody want to add anything?"

Jake McCoy raised his hand.

"Sir, I've said this to Bill and Max, but I want to repeat it here. I know more than a little about staging coups. I also know that democracies like ours, as big and powerful as they are, can be fragile. I think that is what The Seven is counting on. I think when they make their move, they'll do two things simultaneously. One, they'll try to kill as many of the top leaders in the country as they can, including you, Cabinet members, top congressional leaders, and the joints chiefs of staff. This will leave a lot of The Seven members in charge. At the same time, they'll stage a 9/11 kind of event. Maybe several. Amid the chaos and confusion, they will seize power. It could work. Hopefully, the computer file will contain their plans."

Ben Watkins tilted forward in his chair and interrupted.

"But the President is massively protected by the Secret Service."

"Yes, and until just recently three of those massive protectors of the President were members of The Seven, not to mention his press secretary."

Watkins sighed and tilted back.

The President's face was grim as he looked at Bill.

"Bill, is there anything we can do to help Morgen?"

"I don't know, Sir. I'm going to try to call her tonight."

"That's good. Now there's one more thing I want to mention. It's related to what I said at the beginning of the meeting about the importance of maintaining secrecy among us. It is the cold, hard fact that for now we are on our own. We know those lists from Holden aren't complete. That means we're not sure who is part of The Seven and who isn't. We can't trust anybody. Not yet, anyway. We can't even talk about this among ourselves outside of this secure room or another one like it. Waiters and walls have ears. Only if we can find out what The Seven's plans and timeline are, can we make our move. It has to be swift and massive. It will involve the military and every agency of the government. The Seven may be too big for us to take down every member, but we can do what Jake suggests and take out their leaders. Chop the snake's head off. Many of the foot soldiers may get away by simply fading into the woodwork, so to speak. But they'll be harmless without their leaders."

"But what makes you think they'll fade into the woodwork?" Bill asked.

"Because when we move against The Seven, we will do so in a very public and open way. Groups like that function best in the dark. We'll turn the lights on."

There was a short period of silence. The president took a drink of water and continued.

"By the way, Jake. And Ben. Are you going to explain those phones you had trouble getting in here?"

Jake put the cloth bag he had been carrying on the table. He took out the three iPhones and Apple watches. For the next fifteen minutes he described how they worked. He explained that phones number one through four were assigned to Bill, Jake, Max, and Morgen. One, Two, Three, Four. In that order. Alphabetically. The three phones and watches he had brought to Camp David were numbers five, six, and seven.

"Five is for Ben. Six is for Cole. Seven is for POTUS. Again, alphabetical order. These phones allow us to talk privately to one another or to have a private conference call. Because they are encrypted at an extremely high level and operate on WiFi signals instead of cell signals, the calls are virtually impossible to crack. I know, nothing is impossible or perfect. But this encryption is about as close as we can get. If a WiFi signal is password protected, these phones will override the password. If any of you try to call one of us and a stranger answers, hang up. If there's no answer and the person you're calling doesn't call back in a reasonable amount of time, notify the rest of us."

The President held his phone and smiled.

"Jake, where did you get these? I've never heard of anything like them. Does Bob Walker ... oh, sorry. Cole, do you know about these?"

"No, Sir, I don't. Where did you get them, Jake?"

"Look, I was a CIA field agent for thirty years in some strange corners of the world. I know a lot of people you and the President shouldn't even know exist. Just trust me on these phones. They work and will allow us to secretly stay in touch."

The President sighed.

"Okay. No more questions about the phones. Martha, my secretary, is going to wonder where the hell I got an Apple watch. But look, our first job is to get that computer file from New Mexico. Exactly where is that ranch, anyway?"

Bill answered.

"We don't know for sure, Sir. We only know that it's somewhere near the Mexican border. But I'll try to find out from Morgen."

"If she can just give us a general idea, we can find it. There's a command center down the hall with all kinds of maps and computers and links. Cole, you can run that without us having to bring anybody else in, can't you?"

"Yes, Sir. I think so."

"Good. Well, I recommend we take a break for dinner. We can decide later if we want to come back down here tonight or meet in the morning, or both. Everybody's spending the night, right?"

Five heads nodded.

"I asked the cook to fix fried chicken and mashed potatoes. I assume that's okay. Who doesn't like fried chicken? It goes well with the rustic feel of the place. By the way, Bill, I've had you assigned to Dogwood cabin where Anwar Sadat stayed when he was negotiating the Mideast peace accords with President Carter and Menachem Begin in 1978. I thought it would only be fitting since you're working on a book about the Mideast."

"It is, indeed. Thank you, Sir."

The President stood and was followed by the others. Max opened the door for the President and the group filed out of the conference room behind him into the hall and toward the elevator.

At the elevator, Bill pulled the President aside.

"Sir, after dinner could I have a private word with you?"

"Certainly. We can talk in a small office I have off the living room. Are you going to call Morgen before we talk?"

"I'll try. Could I use your office before dinner for the call?"

"Of course, you could. But why don't you just stay down here and make the call. It's way more secure than my little office and has great WiFi."

"I guess you're right. But should we talk in your office?"

"Good point. I'm not used to being so cautious. Let's talk in another little office I have down here. It's as secure as the conference room."

While the others got on the elevator, Bill went back into the conference room and took a seat in the same chair he had used earlier. He pulled out his iPhone and punched the number four. There was no answer. He ended the call and waited for about five minutes. Suddenly, his watch began to vibrate and a four appeared on its face.

"Morgen?"

"Yes, I was in my apartment when you called. I wanted to go to my car to talk. Where are you?"

"At Camp David. In a secure room. We just finished our first meeting. Everyone else is upstairs."

"Bill, I'm afraid. I just found out this afternoon that they want me to go to New Mexico Monday instead of in two weeks. I don't think they suspect anything, but this could mean a change in their plans. I just don't know. But I'm nervous."

"Morgen, get out of there. Come to New York or Washington. We'll hide somewhere. I can't stand the thought of you being in danger."

"Bill, I have to go through with this. We have to get that file. We have to stop them. If they succeed, we have no future. This is our only option, and right now I'm the only one who can get that file. Tom has set it up with Jesse."

"Can't Jesse mail the file to Tom's parents, like he did the manifests and flight data?"

"No, it's too risky to try a second time. Tom had to make up some excuse to leave the ranch when he mailed the manifests and data. He raised a few eyebrows, but they let him do it anyway. They won't do it a second time."

"I guess you're right. I just can't stand the thought of losing you."

"I know. But if we don't follow through on this, all will be lost anyway."

Bill then briefed Morgen on the meeting.

"I'm going to insist we have another meeting after dinner to let everyone know that you're going to New Mexico way sooner than expected. Jake or one of the others may have some ideas. I don't know how late we'll be. I'll call you in the morning. One other thing. Do you know exactly where the ranch is?"

"Not exactly. I was only there once. But I have a general idea. Nearby roads, that kind of thing. It's big. About ten-thousand acres, I think."

Bill wrote down everything Morgen could remember about the ranch's location.

"That's good information. I'll talk to you in the morning."

"Okay. I love you, Bill Sanders."

"I love you, too, Morgen Remley."

When Bill returned to the large living room of Aspen Lodge, he was met with the pleasant aroma of frying chicken from the nearby kitchen. A white-coated steward had set up a bar in front of the fireplace. Next to it was a table covered with an assortment of nuts, crackers, and cheese.

The other five were standing around talking and drinking. Bill walked over to the bar and ordered a vodka martini with an olive.

As he turned around to join the group, he bumped into the President.

"Excuse me, Sir."

"No problem. I've got a tight grip on this drink. Did you reach her?"

"Yes, Sir. We have to have another meeting after dinner."

"I expected as much."

Conversation over dinner was subdued.

Afterward, over strawberry shortcake and coffee, the President told the group they would be meeting again after dinner.

"Let's say in an hour, at eight. That should give us enough time to finish here and allow you to go to your lodge and freshen up. Whatever bags you brought are already at your lodge. One of the stewards will take you there in a golf cart and then pick you up a few minutes before eight. I've asked Cole to stay in one of the spare bedrooms here in Aspen Lodge."

With that, the President drained his coffee cup and stood up.

"See you all downstairs at eight. Bill, if you would come with me."

The others looked puzzled but didn't say anything.

Bill followed the President back across the living room toward the elevator as the others filed outside to board golf carts for their lodges.

Bill and President Stanton got on the elevator and descended to the bunker. The military aide with the Football stayed upstairs in the living room. One Secret Service agent stayed behind at the elevator entrance on the main floor. Another accompanied Bill and the President Stanton to the bunker. Just past the conference room was a door that opened into a small, but fully furnished, office.

The President turned to the agent.

"Jim, would you stay by the elevator, please. Bill and I will be in this office for probably less than half an hour. You can clearly see the hallway and the door to the office."

"No problem, Sir."

The President opened the door and led Bill into the comfortable office. The President sat behind the wooden desk and motioned for Bill to take a seat in a leather-covered chair to the side.

The President said nothing for a few seconds. He seemed

lost in thought.

"You know, Bill, you and I have something in common."

"What's that, Sir?"

"We both lost the loves of our lives. Both died far too young. Your wife was killed in that plane bombing. Mine died from cancer. She died right after I was elected to a second term. I actually thought of resigning, but I realized that would be too self-pitying of me. But you're lucky. You seem to have rebounded with Morgen Remley. It's been a little harder for me. You can understand that it's a little awkward for the President to ask somebody out. Can you imagine taking someone out to a restaurant and being trailed by Secret Service agents and a military aide with nuclear codes? Not to mention the press. And I can't exactly drop into a singles bar. Plus, I'm not really over my wife's death."

"It's been more than three years, Sir, and I'm still not over Jane's death and probably never will be. But, as I explained in our meeting this afternoon, where my relationship with Morgen leads depends on what happens with The Seven. As you know, people don't just resign from that group."

"No, apparently not. Now, Bill, what exactly did you want to talk to me about in private?"

"It's about Morgen, Sir. As I explained in the meeting this afternoon, she and I are in love and trying to make it work. I'm worried about her. When I talked to her before dinner, she told me The Seven is sending her to the New Mexico ranch on Monday instead of two weeks from now. We don't know what that means. Are they moving up their plans? I worry she may be in serious danger. I tried to get her to leave and come to New York or D.C., but she refused. She thinks they would track her down and kill her. She also said that she's the only one who can get that computer file from New Mexico. I asked why the guy there couldn't just mail it like he did the manifests and flight data. She said if he tried to leave the compound again, it would send up a red flag. She's convinced she has to get in there and get the file herself. I think she's right, but it's very risky. I guess I'm asking for your advice."

"Well, if she fled and came here, I could protect her from The Seven. She could stay here at Camp David. This is pretty secure real estate. But she's right. We need her to get that file."

The President paused, leaned back in his chair, and appeared lost in thought. In a few seconds he leaned forward and look directly at Bill.

"I may have an idea or two I've been mulling over. I need to talk to Cole later tonight. In the meantime, let's keep this to ourselves. Tell the group that Morgen will be going to New Mexico but don't mention your concerns. If they ask, let's just say you and I had a private meeting because I wanted to get some insight into your book about the Middle East. We can share everything with them later after I've talked to Cole. Did you get some idea from Morgen just where this ranch is?"

"Yes, Sir. I wrote it all down in a notebook."

"Good. Hang onto it and give it to Cole later. Jake McCoy suggested The Seven may be planning a series of major attacks to sow confusion during and after a series of assassinations. Maybe we can sow some confusion of our own."

✳

The eight o'clock meeting only lasted about thirty minutes.

The president started thing off by explaining his after-dinner meeting with Bill.

"I noticed some quizzical looks when I brought Bill down here after dinner. I simply wanted him to fill me in on his new book about the Middle East. It's called *Power Points*. Right, Bill?"

"Yes, Sir."

"I wanted us to meet in my office down here in case we discussed anything sensitive. And, in fact, we did. I'll let Bill explain."

"Thank you, Mr. President. As I explained in our earlier meeting today, The Seven planned to send Morgen out to the group's New Mexico ranch compound in two weeks. But I talked with her just before dinner and found out that she's going there on Monday. We don't know what this means. Is The Seven moving up Operation Snakebite? How much danger is Morgen in? At first, I wanted to have her leave Maine and come to New York or D.C. But we need her to get that computer file. The computer guy, Jesse Copeland, who has access to the file, is afraid to mail it like he did the helicopter manifests and flight data. He would have to leave the ranch, something he got away with once but probably couldn't a second time."

Jake drummed his fingers on the table's polished surface.

"This makes me nervous. I don't think Morgen is in any greater danger. In fact, I think the fact they are sending her to New Mexico is a sign they trust her. What makes me nervous is that The Seven may be compressing its time frame for action. We thought we had two weeks, maybe more, to stop them. We may have only a few days. We have to move fast. We've got to get that computer file. It's likely to tell us when and how the group will strike. And just as important, it will give up indisputable proof of what these bastards are up to."

The President nodded in agreement before replying.

"One thing I do know is that we need to meet again in the morning. Let's plan on gathering for breakfast at nine and meeting here again at ten."

Chapter 15

The President was pacing in his bedroom. *Jake McCoy is right. Morgen Remley's Monday move to New Mexico is not a good sign. But we can't make a move without more solid information that we're assuming is in that computer file. A wrong or premature move could be fatal for us and the country.*

He suddenly found himself remembering a couple of lines from a T.S. Eliot poem he had read in college:

This is the way the world ends
Not with a bang but a whimper

The President reached for the special iPhone Jake had given him earlier. It was a few minutes after eleven. *Maybe we can create our own bang to avoid a whimper.*

He pressed number six.

"Mr. President?"

"Did I wake you, Cole?"

"No, Sir. I was just getting ready to go to bed."

"Good. Can you meet me and Bill Sanders in my office down in the bunker in twenty minutes?"

"Yes, of course. Why?"

"I'll explain later."

The President then pressed number one.

"Hello. Mr. President?"

"Bill, can you meet me and Cole Favate in my bunker office in twenty minutes?"

"I have to get dressed and ...."

"Go ahead. I'll have a golf cart pick you up in ten minutes.

Be sure and bring whatever information Morgen gave you about the location of the ranch."

The President ended the call and walked over to his bedroom door and opened it. The Secret Service agent sitting in a chair suddenly jumped up.

"Can I help you, Sir?"

"Yes. Get a steward or somebody to pick up Bill Sanders at Dogwood cabin and bring him here as quickly as possible. And be quiet about it. Don't wake anybody up. Bring him to my office in the bunker."

"Yes, Sir. Right away, Sir."

Bill sat in the same leather chair he had used before dinner in the President's office. Cole settled into an identical chair on the other side of the President's desk.

The President spread his hands in a gesture of frustration.

"Gentlemen, Jake McCoy is right. We're in a bind. We need that file and we need it as soon as possible after Morgen gets to New Mexico Monday. The problem is, even if she can get it from that computer guy, how can she deliver it to us? She can't just leave the ranch."

After a period of silence, the President continued.

"I have an idea that's pretty risky, but it might just work. I wanted to discuss it with you two first before taking it to the group. Bill, I wanted you here because you know Morgen and how she might react to what I'm going to propose. I was going to first talk alone to Cole but changed my mind. Cole, I need your military and technical expertise."

Cole looked directly at the President.

"What are you proposing, Sir?"

"Let's take things a step at a time. The first thing I want to know from you is can we reposition a couple of our high-resolution spy satellites so they can pinpoint that ranch and photograph it without anyone knowing exactly what we're doing? Those lists from Senator Holden are incomplete. We're not sure who is involved with The Seven. The last thing we want is for them to know we've put them under surveillance. Can we do that, Cole? Can you do that from the command center here? Tonight?"

Cole crossed his arms over his chest and stared into space. He blinked before responding.

"Technically, it's possible. It might take two or three hours to reposition the satellites, but it could be done. But how can we keep secret that we're photographing the ranch? Too many people would be involved. What would we be looking for?"

"People. Vehicles. Aircraft. Weapons. The lay of the land. Anything that can help us understand the setup there."

"But why do we want that information?"

"One step at a time, Cole."

"Then back to my question. How can we keep what we're doing secret?"

"What if what we want to do is hidden in something bigger?"

"What do you mean, Sir?"

"What if we ask for photographs of the entire border area of New Mexico. We could even include parts of Arizona and Texas. We could say that it's part of a top-secret operation involving the threat of Mideast terrorists coming across our southern border with Mexico. There would be hundreds of pictures. But we could then cherry pick the ones of the ranch, based on the information Morgen gave Bill about its location. Hopefully, nobody outside our little group would know what we were up to."

"It might work."

Bill pulled a ball-point pen from his shirt pocket and clicked it a couple of times before he spoke.

"How does photographing the ranch help up get the computer file? How does it help get Morgen away from The Seven? We can't just attack the place. It's important, but we know it's just one of The Seven's many arms. Attacking them only at the New Mexico ranch could tip our hand, force them to start

Operation Snakebite, and put Morgen in even more danger."

The President smiled.

"Who said anything about attacking them?"

The President, Cole, and Bill left the office and walked down the carpeted hall to the command center. It was locked, but the President opened it with a fingerprint and palm scanner next to the door. Motion-detecting lights flashed on as they entered. There was a small conference table in the middle of the room. On the walls around the table were a dozen high-definition television and computer monitors. There were four computer stations and several large printers.

The President put his hand on Cole's shoulder and squeezed it.

"It's your show now. This is far beyond the abilities of a politician and a writer."

Cole smiled and sat down at one of the computer stations.

"Before I start, Bill, let's go over what information you have on the location of the ranch."

Bill pulled out his notebook and showed Cole a sketch he had made. It was a square.

"The bottom of the square is very near the border with Mexico. The names or numbers of the roads on the north, east, and west sides are here, as best as Morgen could remember them. I'm sure the ranch, which is about ten-thousand acres, is not as square as I've drawn it, but you get the idea."

"Yes. That's good. We shouldn't have any problem finding it."

Cole turned to the computer, booted it up, and entered his security log-in password. It was rejected. He tried again. Again, it was rejected.

"Mr. President, I can't log into these computers."

"Let me try. I have a password they made me memorize that's supposed to work on any secure computer operated by the U.S. government."

Cole moved aside, and the President sat down in front of the computer. He paused for a few seconds to think, then struck eight characters on the keyboard, and hit the enter key. Almost immediately the computer screen came to life.

"Your turn, Cole. That exhausted my computer expertise."

"Sir, I think the satellites you're thinking of are part of what's called the TAURUS system. I'm not sure how many there are, but they're operated and controlled out of Redstone Arsenal in Huntsville, Alabama. That's who we'll have to contact if we want to reposition one or two of them."

"Can't we just call them?"

"Probably. But let me see if I can find out who exactly, or what department, we need to call. Or, better yet, if we can establish a video and audio hookup. This is a different system than I'm used to at the Pentagon. Give me a few minutes to figure some things out."

After about five minutes, Cole was able to establish a video and audio connection with the Pentagon's satellite control center in Huntsville. A very young-looking colonel named Blake McGregor was staring at Cole, whose own image was in a tiny screen within the larger screen in the upper right corner.

"Colonel, this is Colonel Cole Favate with the Defense Intelligence Agency. I'm with the President and contacting you from Camp David. We have a top-secret emergency and need to reposition one and maybe two TAURUS satellites to image the border between New Mexico and Mexico. We also want to include at least twenty-five miles of the Mexico border with Texas and a similar stretch of the border with Arizona."

"Colonel, you must know I can't do that. That could only happen on direct orders from the commanding general here, General Bates."

The President leaned into the computer screen so his image was clearly visible behind Cole's.

"Colonel, this is the President. I'm ordering you to reposition those satellites."

"I'm sorry, Sir, but for security reasons I'm under strict orders to reposition satellites only under the direct order of General Bates. Even if the order comes from the White House, it has to go through General Bates."

"Stand by, Colonel."

The President picked up a red phone.

"White House switchboard. Can I help you."

"This is President Stanton. Get me General Bates in Huntsville."

"Right away, Sir."

In less than half a minute Bates was on the line.

"General, this is Sam Stanton. I'm at Camp David. I need you to reposition one or two of our TAURUS satellites to photograph and maybe video the border area of New Mexico and parts of Texas and Arizona."

"Sir, that's very complicated. Not to mention expensive. And I need to know what this is about. What are we looking for?"

"General, don't try to bullshit me about military spending. This is a top-secret national security operation involving a possible terrorist attack coming from Mexico. Right now, it's on a strictly need-to-know basis. All you need to know at this moment is I want those satellites repositioned. Now. Is that clear?"

"Perfectly, Sir. We're on it. If we can get them repositioned in time, we can get some night shots. But we'll for sure be operational by daylight."

"Good. Please tell your Colonel McGregor to work with Colonel Favate, who is with me here at Camp David. We want those images fed directly to us at the command center here. Understood?"

"Yes, Sir. No problem."

"Thank you, General Blake. And goodnight."

"Goodnight, Sir."

The President turned to Cole.

"That should do it. I'll leave it to you and Colonel McGregor and his people to work out the details. You'll probably have to be here all night. I'm assuming we won't have any decent images to look at until after sunrise. With the time difference, that'd mean eight or later. Hopefully, we have something by the time we meet at ten. Don't hesitate to wake me up for any reason. I'll have some coffee and sandwiches sent down."

"Thank you, Sir."

"Bill, you can do as you please, but I'm going back to bed."

"I think I'll stay here a little while longer in case I can be of any help."

"Okay. See you guys in the morning, if not sooner."

Accompanied by a Secret Service agent who had been waiting outside the door, the President headed for the elevator.

Cole had begun talking to Colonel McGregor, who said two TAURUS satellites were being repositioned and should be ready in a couple of hours. Cole stressed that the first photos should be of New Mexico. Texas and Arizona could come later. The two agreed to delink their computers until the repositioning was complete.

"When the birds are in position, I'll call you."

"Sounds good. Thanks, Colonel McGregor."

Cole double checked to make sure the computers were no longer connected. He also electronically shut down his computer's microphone and put the computer in sleep mode.

Cole smiled at Bill.

"Can't be too safe."

Cole glanced at the now blank computer screen.

"With the New Mexico pictures coming in first, we'll get a look at the ranch sooner."

"Cole, I have a question. If we get hundreds or thousands of pictures from these satellites, not to mention video, how are we going to find the one with the ranch in time for our meeting?"

"From the description that Morgen gave you of the roads surrounding the ranch, it shouldn't be hard. Look at this."

Cole tapped the keyboard and his computer came to life.

He switched to a regular Internet browser and located a detailed map of New Mexico. In a few minutes he was able to locate the roads Morgen had listed. He put his index finger on the computer screen.

"We know the ranch is somewhere in this area. We know it has a helicopter landing pad and, presumably, some kind of communications equipment like a satellite dish. It shouldn't be that hard to find. Now look at this."

Cole shifted to a military site and called up a different map of New Mexico. This one was divided into rectangular grids, each covering about twenty-five square miles.

"The satellite pictures will be sorted by grid."

He pointed to a grid along the border marked 26-AS3.

"Let's zoom in on that one."

Cole and Bill soon realized that the road numbers and names in that grid didn't match what Morgen had given them.

Cole switched to the grid to the left of 26-AS3 and zoomed in.

They quickly recognized the road names and numbers.

"Bingo, Bill! Now we only have to look at the photos of this grid, 27-AS3. Should be a piece of cake."

"And nobody will be the wiser?"

"Nope. They won't have any idea what we're looking at or for."

There was a knock on the door.

Bill opened it and invited in a very sleepy-looking steward with a tray of sandwiches and a pot of coffee.

Bill and Cole chatted as they ate.

"How long have you known the President?"

"For as long as I can remember. We've been best friends since we were kids in Ohio. Sort of like you and your friend in Indiana you tried to help. Although we never drifted away from one another over the years. We've always been close. I was his best man at his wedding. I was with him when his wife died. After he was elected, he always tried to get me to call him Sam or Samuel, but I just couldn't bring myself to do it."

"How come he hasn't made you a general by now?"

"He might've wanted to, but I warned him early on that our friendship could never influence my career. He has honored that. The people I work with also seem to respect that. I like it that way. If I were promoted to general, the buzz would be that it was because of my friendship with Stanton. So, I'll retire a colonel."

"He certainly seems to be a very strong presence. He sure brought that general to heel."

"You don't know the half of it. He's not a man you want as your enemy."

"What do you think is this plan he's concocting?"

"I don't know. We'll just have to wait and see. If we have the pictures of the ranch by the time of our meeting, maybe we'll know then.

"I hope so. I'm really worried about Morgen."

Cole poured more coffee into their cups.

"What about you? I understand you hit the jackpot with writing."

"I've made a good bit of money, for sure. Lots more than if I'd stayed a reporter. Writing suits me. My wife used to say I was a loner and too secretive. She was right."

"It must have been hard to discover that The Seven killed your wife."

"It was and still is. I'll never get over it."

"What about the UFO thing?"

"What about it?"

"I never took UFOs seriously and now here I am working on an operation with a group of people, including the President, who seem to accept their reality."

"Listen, Cole. Everything I've seen and heard in the last year or so leads me to that conclusion. And it's not just what Colonel West told me when we met or what he later wrote in the letter that I got six months after he died. I believe my friend in Indiana was telling the truth when he said he saw a UFO. I think that UFO abducted his daughter. I believe that security guard who said he saw shafts of light around his house was telling the truth. I believe what my friend wrote in those notebooks I found in which he described his childhood experiences of being abducted. Another thing: The question we should be asking is not 'Do you believe in UFOs?' The question should be: 'What do the facts and data support about UFOs?' We're not talking about Santa Claus here. What someone believes about UFOs and aliens is irrelevant. It should be reality, not belief, that we focus on."

"But as you journalists say, isn't that the story? I mean, if UFOs are a reality, doesn't that change everything?"

"It may change everything. It may change nothing. The Seven was established on the premise that acknowledging UFOs and aliens would destroy our social fabric. But the problem is, we can't deal with that until we stop The Seven from letting loose the monster that the group has become over the decades since the end of the Second World War. If the aliens have been here for thousands of years, I guess there's no rush in trying to cope with them. Keep in mind that despite our best efforts to communicate with them, they seem to ignore us unless they think we're threatening them. When they do interact with us, it's only on their terms. We don't know why they're here or what they want. We may never know. They're almost like background noise that you get so used to you hardly notice."

After a couple of hours, the same sleepy-looking steward returned to bring them more hot coffee and take away the sandwich dishes.

As Bill was pouring fresh coffee, he decided he may as well stay in the command center with Cole for the rest of the night.

"Cole, if you have no objections, I ...."

He was interrupted by the sudden buzz of a black phone next to the computer they were using. Cole picked up the receiver and switched on the speaker so Bill could hear the conversation.

"Colonel Favate."

"McGregor here. Just wanted to let you know that the two

TAURUS satellites are in position over the southern border of New Mexico. There is some light cloud cover, so we scrubbed nighttime photos. But those clouds will dissipate as soon as the sun comes up. Our meteorologists say we should start getting some very detailed shots a little after six New Mexico time. We'll start feeding them to you in real time. That would be a little after eight eastern time. Do you know if you're going to want videos? We can also feed those to you in real time."

"Not sure. We'll let you know. Right now, concentrate on the still shots."

"Will do."

"Thanks, Colonel McGregor. Let's resume our computer link at seven eastern time."

"Okay. Talk to you then."

"Goodbye and thanks again."

Cole put the phone down and looked at Bill.

"You were saying?"

"Just that if you have no objections, I'll stay down here the rest of the night. I couldn't sleep if I tried."

"I had hoped you would. When these images start coming in, two sets of eyes are always better than one."

*

A little after eight, the images started coming in. By eight-forty-five, all the grids along the southern border of New Mexico had been downloaded to the command center's hard drive.

Cole switched on a huge high-definition screen on the wall of the command center. He scrolled though several dozen images of the desert until he came to the ones for grid 27-A53. He then zoomed in tight enough that a car on an unpaved road was clearly visible. Bill was astounded at the high resolution of the photos.

"Here we go, Bill. Let's find those roads and highways Morgen gave us and I bet we find the ranch."

They found it in a matter of minutes.

Cole was suddenly excited.

"Look at that. A helicopter landing pad and even a wind-sock. Look at that satellite dish. It's no TV dish or even a commercial communications dish. That's military. The ranch house, barn, and corral all look normal. Maybe a little too neat."

Cole moved the cursor over the picture.

"Notice anything odd, Bill?"

"No. What?"

"No vehicles. No trucks. No nothing. Unless they're in the barn. But I bet people come and go almost exclusively by hel-icopter. Let's look around."

Cole moved the image so they could see the outer edges of the ranch.

"As I suspected. Look. All the roads and bridges have been blocked or bulldozed over. There's no way in or out except by foot, all-terrain vehicle, or helicopter. Also notice that there are no fortifications. No weapons, at least not visible. They're clearly counting on electronic surveillance, isolation, and se-crecy to protect from intruders."

"Morgen said they controlled access to and from the ranch."

"Doesn't look like there's much going on out there this morning. Or, if there is something going on, it's underground and out of sight. We don't need to bother with video."

Cole picked up the black phone and punched in the code for Colonel McGregor at Redstone.

"Colonel McGregor."

"Colonel, this is Colonel Favate at Camp David. The photos came through fine. We won't need the video, but hang onto it just in case."

"Don't worry. We never destroy anything. Should we repo-sition the satellites or leave them for now? We can ways feed you real-time video from them."

"Let me get right back to you on that."

After hanging up the black phone, Cole pulled the iPhone out of his pants pocket and pressed number seven. After a couple of rings, the President answered.

"Yes, Cole?"

"We have the photographs, Sir. Redstone wants to know if we want to keep the satellites in position for future photos or real-time video."

"Yes, we do. Tell them to hold the satellites where they are until I give the order to reposition them. I was just getting ready to meet the others for breakfast. Then we'll meet at ten. Can you have copies of the most important photos ready for the group by then?"

"I think so, Sir."

"Great. Did Bill finally go to bed?"

"No, Sir. He's been here with me all night."

"Oh, really. Well, see you in the conference room at ten. By the way, I read the Daily Brief on my laptop in the bedroom early this morning. Don't worry about a hard copy."

When the President clicked off, Cole turned to Bill.

"You may as well go upstairs and join the group for breakfast. I'll just be printing out copies of these shots after I call McGregor about the satellites."

"Well, okay. If you're sure you don't need help."

"I'm sure. See you at ten."

∗

When Bill stepped out of the elevator on the main floor of Aspen Lodge, the first thing he noticed was the aroma of bacon. When he rounded the corner into the main room, he could see into the dining area. The President, Ben Watkins, Max, and Jake were all seated at the table. Two white-coated stewards were carrying platters of bacon, scrambled eggs, and biscuits to the table, which was already laden with pitchers of various juices and carafes of coffee. A Secret Service agent was standing outside the main door. Bill assumed another one was at the back door.

As Bill walked toward the dining area, the President looked up.

"Bill, come on over and have some breakfast. I trust you slept well. Sadat's ghost didn't disturb you, did he?"

The others smiled, and the President gave Bill an almost imperceptible wink that Bill knew had nothing to do with Anwar Sadat's spirit.

Ben Watkins looked around.

"Where's Cole?"

The President had started to reach for his coffee cup but hesitated.

"He's working on a little project for me. I'll explain when we meet shortly."

Bill sat down at the table and suddenly realized he was hungry, despite the sandwiches earlier.

CHAPTER 16

It was a little after ten when the six gathered for the third time around the conference table in the bunker under Aspen Lodge.

The President was the first to speak.

"We all know the problem. We have to get our hands on that computer file—New Order, or whatever in the hell it's called—without The Seven knowing we have it for at least long enough for us to see if it's what we think it is: the plan for Operation Snakebite. If that file lays out the operations for a coup against the U.S. government, then we have to move fast and hard. It would be the absolute proof we need to go after The Seven for treason with the full force of civilian and military forces and crush it. If the file doesn't do that, we have to regroup and make different plans. But for now, I believe we must proceed on the assumption that the file contains what we think it does. And we must be ready to move fast.

"I've been concocting a plan I want to discuss with you. If Cole looks a little tired, it's because he's been working on it all night. I'm not being secretive or trying to hold back anything, but I haven't said anything to you as a group because I wanted to be sure of some preliminary steps. Overnight, with Cole's help, I ordered the repositioning of some military satellites so that at dawn they could photograph The Seven's ranch in New Mexico. Bill Sanders helped."

Jake McCoy raised his hand.

"Mr. President, how do we know the exact location of the ranch? And wouldn't such an order to reposition those birds tip off somebody in The Seven that we're on to them? We don't know who they are or where they are."

"Good questions. We were able to locate the ranch because of the names and numbers of some nearby roads that Morgen Remley was able to provide to Bill. I don't think they know what we're up to because the excuse I gave for the repositioning order was that I was acting because of a national security crisis involving possible Middle East terrorists on our southern border. I ordered hundreds, maybe thousands, of photos of the border, covering New Mexico and extending into Texas and Arizona. But Cole and Bill had to consider photos only from the sector where they were pretty sure of the ranch's location. In fact, why don't you take it from here, Cole."

"Yes, Sir."

Cole reached toward the floor beside his chair and pulled up a large manila envelope. Inside was a stack of a dozen or so nine-inch by twelve-inch photographs. He gave everyone a copy of the one showing the ranch house, helicopter pad, satellite dish, barn, and corral.

"We're pretty sure this is it. Anybody who's ever worked on a ranch can see that this one is a little too neat and tidy. Then there's the helicopter pad and satellite dish, which is military grade. Notice also the absence of vehicles. No tractors or trucks, unless they're in the barn. No animals. No activity. I'm willing to bet that whatever is going on at this ranch is going on somewhere underground in a bunker not unlike the one we're in."

Then Cole passed around the remaining pictures one at a time.

"I didn't have time to make everyone a copy of these, but they're all pretty much the same. They show the perimeters of the ranch. You can see that roads and bridges have been blocked or bulldozed over. The only ways in and out are by helicopter, foot, or an all-terrain vehicle."

Ben Watkins ran his hand along the edge of one picture.

"So, we've established where the ranch is, and we have photos of it. Why? What's next? How does this bring us closer to getting that file?"

"Morgen can get it from Jesse Copeland, the computer guy at the ranch."

"So, Morgen gets it. What good does that do us if she's trapped at the ranch? We can't just drive in and have her hand it to us."

"Funny you should put it that way, Ben. Actually, I've been formulating a plan that may allow us to do just that, but in a more dramatic fashion."

Everyone at the table looked perplexed. The President continued.

"There hasn't been a lot of publicity about this, but the Air Force has developed a small fleet of pilotless F-16 fighters. They're remotely controlled, like drones. Three of these jets are based at Kirtland Air Force Base in Albuquerque. What if, once we know Morgen has a copy of the file, one of these planes, loaded with some explosives that produce big pyrotechnic displays, were to be crashed on the ranch, close to the house but not close enough to damage it. No one on the ground would know the plane didn't have a pilot. We could then swoop in with helicopters and personnel to secure the area and try to rescue the pilot or recover the body. It would be a perfectly normal and expected reaction to the crash. It would cause a lot of confusion, especially if we stage it at night."

Ben Watkins interrupted.

"But what does that get us?"

Jake McCoy raised his right hand, palm out.

"Let him finish. I think I see where he's going with this."

The President took a sip of water.

"Thanks, Jake. Hear me out. Take notes. Destroy them later. If you see flaws, say so when I'm finished. That's what we're here for. But let me finish."

Ben Watkins flushed.

"Sorry, Sir."

"No problem. In the confusion during the aftermath of the fiery crash, Morgen, who will have been alerted by Bill about our plan, and whoever else is in the ranch house will naturally come outside to see what the hell is going on. Then three or four Black Hawk helicopters carrying a dozen or more Navy SEALs will land. The SEALs will secure the crash site and, if possible, include the ranch house in the secure area. They will push Morgen and any others who came out toward the barn and corral and away from the crash site. This is when Morgen, who will have in her hand a flash drive containing the file, will slip the drive to one of the SEALs. He will immediately get on one of the helicopters and leave the area with the flash drive. Everything after that will be a by-the-book routine handling of a military aircraft crash. It could take several days. But we'll have the file and The Seven won't know it. If it contains what we think it does, we move."

Bill spoke up.

"But, Sir, doesn't this potentially expose us to The Seven? I understand that your story about a terrorist threat on our southern border might not raise any red flags. But after that we get people at Kirtland Air Force Base involved in crashing a plane. Helicopter crews and some SEALs come into the picture. How can we be sure that one or more of them isn't a member of The Seven? What if the SEAL that Morgen slips the flash drive to is one of them? We'll never see the flash drive. Or another one will be substituted for it that just contains innocuous stuff about UFOs. And what about Morgen? Do we just grab the file and leave her there?"

"Good points, Bill. We have to consider them. But it seems to me that at some juncture we're going to have to risk exposure. The problem is to minimize the exposure and get that file. That's why I want the SEALs involved. I think the chances of them being infiltrated by the Seven are pretty small. As for Morgen, I don't see that we have a choice but to leave her at the ranch. If we flew her out, The Seven would know something was up. We'd have to get her out at a later time under different circumstances. This operation is not that time."

In the silence that followed, Bill looked stricken.

Jake leaned back in his chair and rubbed his neck.

"Sir, I think your plan could work. It's not the first time

I've been involved in an operation that used a diversion to get what we wanted. But there's a weak point. That is the point at which Morgen hands the file over to a SEAL. We must not let that happen. We will lose control of it, like breaking the chain of evidence in a criminal case. The only solution is for one of us who Morgen knows, dressed in military gear like the others, to fly in on one of those choppers and get the file directly from Morgen. I think that person should be me. I'm the only one of us with experience in this kind of operation."

For the first time since the meeting started, Max Burris spoke.

"Jake, you have indeed pinpointed a weak spot. But you're in your seventies."

"Well, I think I can still climb into a helicopter and lift a flash drive."

Everyone chuckled.

The President cleared his throat.

"You're right, Max. Jake has identified a weak spot. Sending one of us in is a good idea, it seems to me. Are you sure you're up to this, Jake?"

'Yes, Sir. I am indeed."

Bill raised his hand.

"I want to go, too. With Jake. As backup. I know I don't have any experience, but this is not a combat operation. Like Jake, I can sit in a helicopter and lift a flash drive. That way, Morgen has two people she can pass the drive to."

Jake looked surprised.

"That's not a bad idea."

The President looked concerned.

"I don't know ...."

There was a sudden knock on the door. The President got up and opened it. One of the Secret Service agents was standing there.

"Sir, you have a call upstairs from the CIA director. He says it's important."

"Have it transferred to the phone down here."

"Yes, Sir."

The President closed the door and walked back to his chair. He picked up a black phone from a credenza behind his chair. He placed the phone on the table in front of his chair and sat back down.

When the phone buzzed, the President put his fingers to his lips to signal silence and switched on the speaker phone.

"Mr. President?"

"Yes, Bob. What can I do for you?"

"Sorry to disturb you, Sir. But I wanted to tell you that in less than two weeks—a week from next Thursday, to be exact—we're having a special training session for a class of new recruits, and we would love for you to attend. It's going to be at our new training center in Maryland. In fact, it's not too far from Camp David. Do you think you could make it?"

"Possibly, Bob. But let me check with Martha in the morning. I won't be going back to the White House until later today."

"Great. Hope you can make it. Your presence would be a heck of a surprise for our guys."

"Thanks for the invite. Anything else, Bob?"

"No, Mr. President. That's it. Thank you. Hope you're having a relaxing weekend."

"I am. Goodbye, Bob."

"Goodbye, Sir."

The President looked around the table.

"Well?"

Max spoke first.

"That was a very weird call, Mr. President. Why would Robert Walker call you here on Sunday morning for such a mundane and routine request?"

"I agree. I think The Seven is planning to make a move a week from Thursday, and they want me out of Washington. We have to move now to get that file. Let's shoot for Wednesday night. Bill and Jake, I think you're both right. We can't screw up getting that flash drive. I want the two of you with the SEALs when they hit the ranch."

CHAPTER 17

The President stood up, then motioned for everyone else to remain seated.

"First of all, Bill, Jake, and Cole, I want the three of you to stay at the White House until this is over. There's plenty of room in the residence. You can flip a coin to see who gets the Lincoln Bedroom. Bill and Jake will be flying, probably early Wednesday, to New Mexico to meet up with the SEALs. Cole will work out the details. Max and Ben, I want you close at all times. But sleep in your homes, which aren't that far from the White House, so as not to arouse unnecessary suspicion. I can't emphasize enough the importance of keeping this from the press.

"Max, Ben, and I will fly back shortly. Cole, why don't you leave about an hour after I do? Bill and Jake can leave in another hour or so, just don't leave at the same time."

Max turned to the President.

"Sir, where are we going to be able to meet in the White House that we can be certain is secure?"

"I've been thinking about that. I can make the Oval Office dark, but I'm not sure how much I trust that feature after those three Secret Service agents. No reflection on you, Ben."

"I understand, Sir."

"Another possibility is the Situation Room. It's supposed to be secure, but it's loaded with high-tech electronics that make me nervous. I think maybe we should meet outside on the Truman Balcony. With drinks. It would look perfectly normal. We can set up a CD player with an opera turned up just loud enough to obscure our voices. Yes, let's do that. Let's plan on meeting on the balcony at six tonight and Monday night for cocktails before dinner. Anybody object to *Aida*?"

The others smiled and nodded.

"One more thing. Bill, you've got to call Morgen and fill her in on what we know and are planning so far. Details may change, but right now we're going to try to crash the F-16 Wednesday night. We can give her the exact time later."

"I was expecting to do that, Sir."

"Okay, let's adjourn for now. I'll see you at the White House later today. We're on our own. We need to stay close. And let's not talk about any of this while we're socializing. Let's only talk when we're sure of security. By our meeting tomorrow evening, I expect Cole will be able to update us with some solid plans. On the way back to Washington, I'm going to call the Chief of Naval Operations and the Air Force Chief of Staff from Marine One and tell them that Cole is in charge of a top-secret anti-terrorist operation along the Mexican border that will involve Kirtland and Holloman. I will emphasize that it's on a strict need-to-know basis, and that until further notice an order from Cole is to be treated as an order from me. I'll instruct them to pass these orders down to the officers and enlisted men at both bases, as well as the SEALs involved in the operation."

Bill, Jake, and Cole shielded their eyes from the blast of wind as Marine One lifted off from the Camp David helipad, banked, and turned south toward Washington.

Cole sighed.

"This all seems kind of unreal. I feel like I'm in a bad dream."

Jake put his hand on Cole's shoulder.

"It's not a dream. Too much reality for that. Too many bodies."

"I know."

Bill remained silent as they started walking toward Aspen Lodge.

✳

After Cole had left the compound, Bill and Jake sat at the dining room table. A steward offered them lunch, but they declined.

"Jake, why don't you leave first. Then I'll go down in the bunker and call Morgen."

"Fine. But I wanted to talk to you before you call Morgen. Let's talk downstairs, just to be safe."

They took the elevator to the bunker where a Secret Service agent escorted them into the conference room. He closed the door as he left. The room seemed bigger with only the two of them there. They sat on opposite sides of the table.

"What did you want to talk about?"

"Stanton doesn't have a military background, but he's a good politician and a good thinker. I think his plan will work. But I want you and I to modify it slightly when we're on the ground at the ranch. And keep it among you, Morgen, and me."

"Modify it how?"

"Well, the plan as it was outlined calls for Morgen to hand me the flash drive during all the confusion. But I've done operations like this before. We need to make it a little more complicated and distracting, just in case something goes wrong. Or in case one of those SEALs is involved with The Seven. Remember how magicians work? They distract their audience. You're focused on the spinning plate or silk scarf and you don't see what the magician is really up to that makes his tricks work. We need another layer of distraction in case one of those SEALs or other crew members are part of The Seven and see Morgen hand me something."

"So, what do we do?"

"You need to tell Morgen to bring two flash drives. One empty, the other containing The New Order file. Make certain she can tell them apart in the dark. It won't be totally dark, what with flashlights and whatever lights are probably on the barn. But it might be dark enough to cause confusion if we're not careful. Tell her to use flash drives that are different sizes. Or maybe stick a piece of tape on one. Have her pass the empty one to me. I'll then create a distraction of some sort and then she can pass the one containing the goodies to you. If someone tries to take the flash drive from me, all they'll get is nothing. If this works, no one will know that Morgen passed the real one to you. It gives us an extra layer of security."

"What kind of distraction will you create before Morgen hands me the drive?"

"I haven't figured that out yet. But remember my friends in low places. I'll have something, and it'll be good."

"I believe you."

"I guess I should get started for D.C. Since I'll be arriving at the White House before you, I'm claiming the Lincoln Bedroom."

"Go for it. I'll call Morgen from here and should be an hour or so behind you."

As soon as Jake left the conference room, Bill called Morgen. There was no answer.

He waited.

In less than five minutes his watch began to vibrate and the number four appeared on its face.

"Morgen. Where are you?"

"I'm in my car as usual. Just outside the apartment."

"Are you still going to the New Mexico ranch tomorrow?"

"Yes. A private plane is picking me up at the Portland airport at nine in the morning. I'm flying to Las Cruces and from there will fly to the ranch in a helicopter."

Bill spent the next quarter hour or so filling Morgen in on the group's plans.

"I'll call you later about the exact time Wednesday night when the jet will be crashed. But in case we can't connect, I'm pretty sure it's going to be ten or ten-thirty. You won't have any trouble getting outside for a call, will you? Maybe late

Monday or early Tuesday."

"No. The place is so isolated and electronically protected that they don't worry about people running off. They can easily track us. Where would any of us go anyway? What's this distraction Jake is going to cause right after I hand him the phony drive?"

"I don't know. But Jake's an operator. I'm sure it'll be something attention grabbing."

"We'll just have to wait and see."

"Morgen, there's one other thing we need to discuss."

"What?"

"I tried to convince Stanton and the group that we should pull you out of there with us Wednesday night. They all disagreed, especially Stanton. He thinks that would tip our hand to The Seven. They want you to stay behind and be taken out at a later time. It wouldn't be much later because, as I said earlier, everything is going to come to a head by a week from Thursday if we're reading that call from Walker correctly. We'll know when we get the file."

"I've been expecting that, and I agree with Stanton and the others. If we slip the file out without them knowing, I don't think I'll be in any danger."

"I guess I don't have any choice but to go along with that. But if anything goes wrong, I'm dragging you to the closest Black Hawk."

"You won't have to drag me. You'll have to catch up with me."

"Morgen, I think this is going to work. And if the file is as incriminating as we think it is, The Seven will be finished. The President will do whatever it takes, and that can include a lot."

"I know. But I'd be lying if I said I wasn't a little scared."

"I know. So am I. I'm a writer, not a warrior. What if I drop that flash drive? Or trip? Or wet myself?"

Morgen laughed.

"You won't do any of those things. You know why? Because I love you and you love me, and when this is all over, we'll be able to be together and forget about The Seven. Not UFOs and aliens but at least The Seven."

"God, Morgen, I love you."

"I love you, too."

✳

When Bill arrived at the White House, he was ushered in without any trouble and directed to park his rental car in a space between the executive mansion and the Eisenhower Executive Office Building. After getting his suitcase and overnight bag out of the trunk and locking the car, he was approached by a uniformed Secret Service agent and a steward, who took his luggage.

The agent motioned toward a side door of the West Wing.

"Follow me, Sir. The President is expecting you. He's in the residence on the second floor."

Once inside the West Wing, the uniformed agent handed Bill over to a plainclothes agent who led Bill from the West Wing to the main White House. An elevator whisked them to the second floor, where Bill was greeted by Max.

"Welcome, Bill. No problems I trust."

"None at all."

"Well, come on. Everybody's in the kitchen drinking beer."

Ben Watkins, Cole, Jake, and the President were seated around an island in a kitchen that was jarringly modern compared with the rest of the second floor. Although Bill had covered the White House for several years when he was a reporter, he had only been in the residence very briefly a couple of times.

The President looked up as Bill and Max entered the kitchen.

"Bill, welcome. Help yourself to a beer. There're several kinds in the refrigerator. There's also cheese and crackers and some potato chips here."

"Thank you, Sir. I think I will."

Bill opened the refrigerator door and pulled out a

Heineken. A white-jacketed steward took it from him, whipped the condensation off with a white towel, opened it, and handed it back to him with a napkin.

"I tried to tell Adalberto that this was informal, but he just can't help himself."

Adalberto smiled at the President and gathered up some empty beer bottles from the island.

Bill pulled an empty stool up to the island and sat down across from Cole, Ben, and Jake. Max was to his left and the President to his right.

"Bill, we're putting you in one of the guest bedrooms. The first thing Jake said when he walked in here was that he wanted the Lincoln Bedroom."

"No problem, Sir. We already discussed that."

"Gentlemen, I propose that as soon as we finish here, we take a break and get ourselves ready for dinner. If you need anything, just ask Adalberto. Max and Ben, if you want to go home for an hour or so, take a White House car and driver. It's a little after four now. Let's meet for drinks on the balcony at six. We'll eat around seven or seven-thirty, depending on how things go. We're having pot roast and cherry pie with vanilla ice cream for dessert. That okay with everybody?"

Five heads nodded in unison.

"Good. It's great to have some company up here. You have no idea how many nights I eat alone."

✳

Max and Ben had decided to stay at the White House since they both would be going home after dinner.

At six, everyone moved out on to the Truman Balcony with its commanding view of the Washington Monument. Adalberto has set up six cushy lawn chairs in a semicircle facing the monument. On one side was a bar; on the other a table with a Bose CD player next to a stack of CDs. A second steward, who had come from downstairs, was tending bar and would later help Adalberto serve dinner.

The President introduced him.

"Gentlemen, this is Ralph Logan. He's mixed drinks for four presidents. Democrats and Republicans. He knows what he's doing. Just tell him what you want."

Ralph turned to the President.

"You first, Sir."

"Scotch and soda, please."

"Right away, Sir."

As the others got their drinks and began to settle into the chairs, the President walked over to the CD player, picked up a disc from the stack, and lifted it out of its plastic case.

"*Aida* still okay with everybody?"

Without waiting for an answer, the President inserted the disc and punched the play button. After the overture had been playing for a few seconds, the President adjusted the volume loud enough to cover their conversation.

"I don't think any of the neighbors will object."

The President nodded at Ralph, who, with Adalberto, went into the residence and closed the doors to the balcony.

The President raised his drink in a toast.

"Well, gentlemen, here we are. I'm sorry Morgen can't be with us. She has the most important role of all. Plus, I'm anxious to meet her. Anyway, let's look at what progress we've made so far. Cole?"

"Sir, I've been able to get some things in place today. Everything will be firmed up in the morning. I've used the same cover story we used to reposition the TAURUS birds: We're involved in a highly classified operation to intercept a group of Mideast terrorists we think are trying to cross our southern border. They may have Stinger missiles and be capable of bringing down commercial or military aircraft. The pilotless F-16 from Kirtland will be crashed at the coordinates I worked out and had double checked. I'll know for sure in the morning, but as it stands now the F-16 will go down at ten-thirty Wednesday night. It'll be carrying lightweight explosives that will produce more noise and light than damage. Also, tomorrow we're moving four Black Hawks and twenty-four SEALs to

Holloman Air Force Base in Alamogordo, north of the ranch. Three of the choppers will arrive at the ranch about twenty minutes after the F-16 goes down. The fourth chopper will lag ten or fifteen minutes behind the other three as a backup or to jump in if something goes wrong. Of course, the TAURUS birds are constantly monitoring the ranch in real time. So far, there's been almost no activity there. Today we saw one guy, who looked like a worker, walk out to the barn and back to the house in a few minutes. If things are as slow there as it appears, that's greatly to our advantage. I've also arranged to have a secure computer set up at Holloman. That's so we can quickly get the file on the flash drive in President Stanton's hands here so he can read it and make a decision to move."

The President interrupted.

"And move fast if that file is what we think it is. Things should be pretty much in place when we meet here at the same time tomorrow. Bill and Jake, you two need to be prepared to travel at a moment's notice, depending on what Cole works out. Great work, Cole."

"Well, Sir, it's amazing what a lowly colonel can do when it's clear the President has his back."

Jake spoke for the first time since they had come out to the balcony.

"Sir, if that file contains what we think it does, what will you do?"

"I haven't fully decided yet. It will certainly involve an address to the nation. This is the kind of stuff I ought to be hashing out with my staff, but right now I'm afraid to go beyond our group. Don't worry. Whatever I do will be forceful and conclusive. In fact, Bill, I might ask you to help me write the address. Would you do that?"

"Of course, Mr. President."

"Even if it gets you involved in a shitstorm? Oh, hell, you're already involved."

"Yes, I am. Deeply."

The President got up and freshened his drink at the bar.

"One other thing. I'm going to call Bob Walker at CIA in

the morning and tell him I'm coming up to the training exercise next week. Make them think whatever they're planning is working. If things go as we expect, this should all be over well before then. But this is a tough one for me. I've known Bob for a long time. We were roommates at Ohio State. What the hell was he thinking to get involved in something like this?"

The question hung in the air.

Cole broke the silence.

"There's one thing I was going to mention earlier, but I got sidetracked. I'm flying to Holloman with Bill and Jake, and then I'm flying to the ranch on one of the Black Hawks with them. The reason is that when we get back to Holloman, I want to be the one controlling that flash drive and getting its contents into that secure computer and on the way to the White House."

The President looked at Jake.

"You're a pro. What do you think?"

"I agree with Cole. He's military. He's operating under Presidential authority. He'll be in command. Plus, he knows how to operate a secure computer. That means we don't have to go outside our group for an important step."

"I agree. Gentlemen, I think dinner will be ready in a few minutes. Is there anything else we need to discuss? We won't get a chance to really talk again until tomorrow at six."

Bill let his gaze drift to the Washington Monument and the deepening shadows around the White House.

"I think there is something we need to discuss, Sir. But maybe not at the tail end of a meeting when dinner is waiting. It's the reality of UFOs, or UAPs, whatever you call them, and the aliens that control them. What are we going to do about that? The government's been covering the whole thing up since the 1940s. If we expose and destroy The Seven, what happens to the coverup? Do we continue it somehow or do we come clean? What are the consequences of either move?"

"You're right, Bill. We need to have that discussion. Let's do it tomorrow evening. That gives us all time to sleep on it."

Ben Watkins, who had been silent, raised both hands and looked skyward.

"Christ Almighty! If somebody had told me a week ago that I'd be here tonight discussing this, I would have told them to stop drinking and see a shrink."

＊

Bill was standing on the Truman Balcony. It was a dark, moonless night. The lights atop the Washington monument looked like two red eyes in a head covered with a pointed hood. Distant sounds seemed muted.

"Hello, Bill."

Bill turned to see Colonel Richard West sitting in one of the chairs the group had used earlier. He was wearing the same dark brown suit and green tie he had worn when they met more than a year ago.

"Why don't you stay the fuck dead!"

West grinned and pointed out to the South Lawn. There was the President, Morgen, and Jake, standing side by side and looking stiff and lost.

Bill started to shout and wave at Morgen, but she seemed not to hear or see him. He turned around.

West was gone. In the chair where he had been was Cindy Watson. She was wearing the green pajamas that she was wearing when she was abducted more than a year ago in Indiana.

She looked directly at Bill.

"Be careful, Mr. Sanders."

Bill looked back out at Morgen and the other two, still standing stiffly next to each other.

When Bill turned back to Cindy, she was gone. Vanished.

Suddenly, the wind picked up. From somewhere above came a loud booming noise. It was gone as quickly as it came, followed by an eerie silence.

Bill turned toward the South Lawn again.

He watched, frozen, as a large triangular craft settled silently over the White House grounds. Neither Morgen, the President, nor Jake seemed to notice.

From the center of the craft, a shaft of intense blue light sliced through the dark, illuminating the three. In a few seconds they began to rise through the air and the blue light toward the craft. In less than a minute they were gone. The ship suddenly vanished. Normal noises of the city returned.

Hot tears welled up in Bill's eyes.

Bill jolted awake and sat bolt upright in bed. At first, he was confused, not sure where he was. Then as the intensity of the dream began to fade, he realized he was in a guest bedroom in the White House, just two doors from the President's bedroom. Jake was in the Lincoln Bedroom. Cole was in another guest room. He lay back on the pillows and tried to relax. *Jane had not appeared in the dream. Maybe that was a good sign.* After about twenty minutes, he fell back asleep.

✳

Bill was awakened by a knock on the bedroom door.

"Yes?"

"It's Adalberto, Sir. There's a buffet breakfast in the kitchen whenever you're ready."

"What time is it?"

"Almost eight, Sir."

"Okay. Thanks."

Bill showered, shaved, and dressed. He was unsure what to wear; he settled for slacks, loafers, and a dress shirt, open neck with no tie.

When he walked into the large kitchen, the President, Max, and Cole were already there. He sat down at the island next to Max.

Adalberto was pouring coffee and various kinds of juices. There were several warming trays loaded with scrambled eggs and bacon, as well as eggs benedict and hash browns. A square tray was filled with several boxes of cold cereal.

The President and Max were dressed in business suits and ties. Cole wore his Air Force uniform.

The President smiled at Bill.

"I trust you had a good night's sleep, Bill."

"I did indeed, Sir." *Except for that dream.*

"Good. Help yourself. If you don't see something you like, just tell Adalberto."

"Oh, no. This is perfect, Sir. Where's Jake?"

"Here I am."

Jake walked into the kitchen. He was dressed in slacks and an open-neck shirt like Bill.

The President pointed to the food.

"Help yourself. I trust you slept well. Mr. Lincoln's ghost didn't disturb you?"

"Nope. I slept like a baby."

After everyone had eaten and were working on their second or third cup of coffee, the President stood up, motioning for the others to remain seated.

"Max, Cole, and I have day jobs. Bill and Jake, what are you going to do today until we meet at six on the balcony?"

"Later in the day I need to call Morgen when she gets to the ranch. I also need to call my agent in New York. Other than that, not much. If I had my laptop, I could write. But it's just as well I don't. I'm a little wired for writing at the moment. What about you, Jake?"

"Free as a bird. I thought we might have lunch somewhere."

The President took a last sip of coffee.

"Look, if you two leave the White House grounds, I want you to be under Secret Service protection. I've already arranged it with Ben. If you want to go anywhere, they'll drive you. At this point, I don't want to take any chances. Max, Cole, and I will be in the West Wing. You can always reach us with those incredible phones Jake gave us. I'm beginning to like this Apple watch, by the way. It even tells me the phase of the moon and the outside temperature."

With that, the President walked out of the kitchen and headed toward his bedroom.

"Max, Cole, I'll meet you at the elevator in five minutes."

Two Secret Service agents who had been waiting in the

center hall moved toward the elevator. They were joined by a military aide carrying the forty-pound case containing the nuclear launch codes.

Except for two maids and two stewards, Bill and Jake were alone in the residence.

Jake looked out the curved window overlooking the West Wing and the Eisenhower Executive Office building.

"Well, Bill, it looks as if you and I have a couple of empty days ahead of us."

"I need to call my agent. I'll be right back."

Bill walked to his bedroom and closed the door. He started to use his cell phone but stopped, wondering if it could somehow tip off The Seven. He remembered that the iPhone Jake gave him was encrypted, but only for calls to members of the group.

There was a White House phone on the table next to his bed. He picked up the receiver.

"White House switchboard. How can I help you, Mr. Sanders?"

Bill was momentarily startled that the operator knew his name. But then he realized that the same thing would have happened if he had been in a hotel.

"I need to call a number in New York, but I don't want them to know I'm calling from the White House."

"No problem, Sir. I'll put you through on a secure line that will simply say 'Unknown Caller' if they have caller ID. What's the number?"

Bill gave the operator Nancy's office number.

Nancy's assistant answered.

"Hi. It's Bill Sanders. Is Nancy in?"

"Oh, Mr. Sanders. She just got in. Hold on please."

In a few seconds Nancy was on the line.

"Bill, where are you?"

"In D.C."

"Are you okay?"

"I'm fine."

"Are you any closer to resolving the issues from your trip to Indiana last year?"

"Yes, I think so. That's why I called. I may have things wrapped up within the week and be back in New York writing. Then I'll be able to explain everything to you, as I've promised more than once."

"That's great news."

"There's something else."

"What?"

"Depending how things go, I may be proposing a book based on my experiences that started with that trip to Jefferson. I want you to think about the possibility that the book could be huge. Bigger than anything I've ever done. Big enough that we may want to figure out a way to postpone *Power Points* and do this one first."

"Oh, Bill, I don't know. We could wind up in a legal fight with your publisher. *Power Points* is a sure thing for them. They have a contract with you. They aren't going to give it up without a fight."

"They wouldn't be giving it up. Only delaying it."

"That's a tall order. You're asking a lot."

"I know. But all I want you to do now is consider it. And keep an open mind. When you hear details of what I've been dealing with after it's resolved, I think you'll want to find a way to make it work. Please, just think about it for now."

Nancy's voice was tense and strained.

"I will. You know I trust you."

"Thanks, Nancy. I'll call you when I get back to New York in a week. Maybe by the weekend."

Bill opened his bedroom door and walked out into the center hall of the residence. Jake, sitting in a blue wingback chair, was reading a book.

"Where'd you get the book?"

Jake pointed across the hall.

"Over there. There's a library."

Suddenly the elevator door opened, and a Secret Service agent stepped out. Both Bill and Jake recognized him but didn't know his name.

"Gentlemen, I'm agent Roger Yates. I wanted to check with you and see what you're planning for today. As I believe you know, President Stanton wants you protected by our agents if you leave the grounds of the White House. We will drive you anywhere you want to go."

Jake lay the book on a table next to his chair.

"I was just about to ask Bill if he would like to take a walk and then get some lunch somewhere later."

"That's fine. Another agent and I will accompany you, but at a discreet distance."

Jake turned to Bill.

"That okay with you?"

"Sure. I could use some exercise."

After lunch, Bill and Jake sat on an isolated park bench near Dupont Circle. The Secrets Service agents were standing nearby but well out of hearing range.

"Bill, we need to change our plans a bit."

"Why? How?"

"Remember, Morgen is to hand me the empty flash drive and then, while I create a distraction, pass the real one to you?"

"Yes. So?"

"Well, now that Cole Favate is going to be with us, we need to include him in our little ruse. He needs to know what we're doing, and you need to pass the drive to him. He's the one who will then take it back to Holloman and get its contents to Stanton. We'll fill him in on our way out there tomorrow or Wednesday. We should know which day we're flying out after we meet tonight."

"You're right, of course. I never thought about it."

"Good. Well, I don't know about you but by the time we

walk back to the White House, I'm going to be ready for a nap."

"Not a bad idea."

✳

Later in the afternoon, Bill was stretched out on his bed, half awake and half asleep, when his watch started to vibrate. It was Cole Favate.

Bill reached for his iPhone on the bedside table.

"Cole?"

"Bill, I wanted to let you know that Morgen just arrived at the ranch. One of our TAURUS birds videoed her helicopter landing. She and an unidentified male got out and walked into the ranch house. The chopper then left. I can show you the video if you want."

"No, I don't need to see it. I'm going to try to call her in a half hour or so. Do you know yet the exact time the F-16 will crash Wednesday night?"

"Yes. Ten-thirty."

"That's what I estimated the last time she and I talked. But I need to confirm it with her."

"Are you sure you can call her without any problems?"

"I think so. She told me they don't care if she goes outside. For fresh air or whatever. I'm not sure what the range of their WiFi signal is, so she may have to stay close to the house. It'll be a quick conversation. Once she knows the exact time for sure, I won't have to call her again."

"If you need me for anything, give a call. Otherwise, I'll see you at six on the balcony with the others."

Bill lay back on the bed. *Maybe I shouldn't call Morgen so soon after her arrival at the ranch. Maybe I should wait until tomorrow.*

He got up, went into the bathroom, washed his face, and changed shirts.

There was a knock on the door.

"Yes?"

"It's Adalberto, Sir. I just wanted to see if you needed any-thing. We'll be starting to prepare dinner soon."

"Thanks, but I'm fine."

"Very well, Sir. Just let me know if you need anything."

"I will. Thanks again."

Bill looked at his watch. Four-thirty.

He picked up his iPhone and punched the number four. No answer.

Ten minutes later, his watch vibrated. It was Morgen.

"Morgen, are you all right?"

"Yes, fine. I just got here less than an hour ago. Some man I never met before came with me. He said his name was Ray. Never gave his last name. We hardly spoke the whole trip. He is very tall and thin, and his head is shaved bald. He was also carrying a gun in a shoulder holster that he made no effort to conceal. As soon as we got here, he and Jesse Copeland pretty much ignored me and started going over computer data. I'm still not exactly sure why they sent me here other than something about crunching computer data. But I think the answer may come from the mystery man I flew here with. Right now, I'm walking around outside the house. The WiFi signal is strong."

'Morgen, the F-16 will crash Wednesday night at ten-thirty. Within twenty minutes three Black Hawk helicopters full of Navy SEALs will arrive. In the confusion, you can pass the fake drive to Jake. When he springs his diversion, give me the real one."

"I understand. We went over this in our last call. I just needed the exact time. I'll get the flash drives from Jesse tonight or tomorrow."

"I know. I'm just nervous and worried. I probably shouldn't try to call you tomorrow, but what if something happens and you can't get the flash drive? How will we know?"

"Look, as soon as I get the drive, I'll call you twice in a row, short calls about thirty seconds apart. Don't answer. Twice means I have it. Three calls in a row means there's a problem."

"That should work. But I still don't want to leave you there."

"We have to, Bill. It's the only way. You know that. Our future depends on it."

"I know."

"I better get back inside."

"You know I love you, don't you, Morgen?"

"Of course, I know that. I love you, too."

✳

When the drinks had been served and the doors to the Truman Balcony closed, the President inserted a CD into the player.

"It's *Carmen* tonight. By the way, for dinner we're having grilled salmon and shrimp scampi."

He sat down and looked around at the others as the overture to *Carmen* started. The President adjusted the volume to make it a bit louder.

"I would like Cole to go first and fill us in on Wednesday's plans, which I think are complete. Then I want us to discuss the larger issue of UFOs and aliens that Bill brought up last night. Does anyone want to say anything or ask a question before Cole starts?"

Bill raised his hand slightly. The President nodded toward him.

"I spoke with Morgen a little over an hour ago. She is at the ranch. Cole had told me earlier that the F-16 would crash at ten-thirty. I passed that on to her. She told me that on the flight she was accompanied by a tall, thin man carrying a gun who said his name was Ray. He didn't say much else. Gave no last name. She's not sure what he's doing there. May have to do with computers. Morgen said she would get the flash drives from Jesse Copeland tonight or tomorrow."

Jake turned to Bill.

"What if there's a problem in her getting the drives? Shouldn't we confirm she has them before we start the operation?"

"We've worked out a signal by which she'll let me know if

she has the flash drive or if there's a glitch ...."

Bill's watch started to vibrate and display the number four. He held up his index finger to indicate silence. The watch stopped vibrating and the face returned to its normal watch mode. Thirty seconds later, it began to vibrate again and display a four. In a few seconds, the vibrating ended, and the normal watch face appeared.

Bill again indicated for everyone to be silent.

Three minutes went by and there was no third call.

"Morgen has the flash drive. If not, she would have made a third call."

The other five broke into applause.

The President reached over and patted Bill on the shoulder.

"Very good. Now we just have to get the damn thing. Where are we on that, Cole?"

"I think all the pieces are falling into place, Sir. The remote flight crews at Kirtland are ready to crash one of those F-16 loaded with some light bombs onto the ranch just a few hundred yards north of the house. All that the commander and crews at Kirtland know is that this is a top-secret operation approved by the White House against some terrorists who are trying to cross into the United States from Mexico. By tomorrow afternoon, twenty-four Navy SEALs and four Black Hawks will be in place at Holloman. Three of the choppers and eighteen SEALS will arrive at the ranch twenty minutes after the F-16 crashes. As I indicated earlier, the fourth chopper will lag ten or fifteen minutes behind the others as backup. Again, all any of them know is that they're on a mission involving suspected terrorists. Bill, Jake, and I will fly to Holloman Wednesday morning from Andrews. Oh, there's one other thing. When I send the flash drive's file from the secure computer I've had set up at Holloman, it will have to go to a computer in the White House Situation Room. I know, Mr. President, that you have some concerns about that room. But trying to do anything else would have involved too many other people and taken too long. It's a small risk I think we just have to take."

The President smiled.

"That's fine, Cole. I think I was being a little paranoid about the Situation Room. Just call me when you're ready to send the file, and I'll go down there to personally receive it. If it's what we think it is, things will happen so fast that security will be less of a concern."

Jake raised his glass in a toast to Cole.

"Sounds to me like you've got everything pretty much under control."

"I hope so."

"I just have one question for the President. Sir, if that flash drive contains the proof that we think it contains of a coup against the United States, what exactly are you going to do?"

"I've been thinking about that a lot, Jake. While the decision is ultimately mine, under normal circumstances I would be getting advice from national security aides, the intelligence community, and the military. But we know I can't do that because we won't know for sure where The Seven's tentacles reach. My own press secretary, for Christ's sake. So, I'm going to have to decide pretty much alone what action to take. But I can tell you this: If that document we're trying to get is the proof that I need, I will move against these people with more force than they can imagine. Remember, gentlemen, laws passed after 9/11 give the President some pretty extraordinary power. I will use it to save this country and its government. And rest assured, Bill, that I will also do everything in my power to rescue Morgen. So, stand by."

Conversation stopped for a minute or so as *The Toreador Song* reverberated across the Truman Balcony.

The President stood up.

"We better refresh out drinks before we go on. Our next topic is a big one."

After the drinks were served, the President motioned to Bill.

"As you have urged, Bill, let's discuss the UFO thing. What do we do about that? I know that ultimately, the decision and responsibility are mine, but I'd sure love some advice. Especially from you. After all, it was your trip to Indiana last year that led to uncovering the whole unnerving business with The Seven. This is a separate issue from the bastards' coup plans."

"The decision you have to make, Sir, is what to do with the truth about, and reality of, UFOs and aliens when we expose The Seven. Do we continue the original coverup that Truman started, or do we come clean with our fellow citizens and the world? According to Colonel West, you're only the third President since Truman to know the truth. But you discovered it. It wasn't revealed to you by The Seven as it apparently was to Kennedy and Reagan. Why those two remains a mystery. Since the end of the Second World War, there have been dozens of studies by NASA and think tanks large and small, including Brookings and RAND, about what should be done if the government had proof of UFOs and alien visitations. Virtually all of these concluded that the government should keep a lid on it because of the social, psychological, and civil disruptions that would result. Especially since the government doesn't have a clue who the aliens are or what they're up to. Thus, The Seven's efforts to both ridicule UFOs and at the same time create the illusion that the government knows what's going on and keeps it a secret. The Seven's goal over the decades has been to protect the status quo. I'll never forget Colonel West's words to me about this in our meeting last year: *Can you imagine what would happen if we were to confirm that UFO sightings and aliens are real? What if we said to the public: Yes, these craft and beings from we-don't-know-where routinely invade our air space, kidnap our citizens, mutilate our cattle—and we know nothing about the who or the why of any of this. We are powerless, absolutely powerless, to do anything. We don't know whether they are here for good or for evil reasons. And, oh, by the way, we suspect they can read our minds and might be altering our genetic makeup. Can you imagine what would happen to the fabric of society? To religions? To government institutions? To government authority? To the stock market?* In his letter to me that arrived six months after he died, West had changed his mind."

Ben Watkins broke in.

"Shouldn't we take the conclusions of these major think tanks seriously? After all, we don't want to save our country from a coup only to see its social order ripped apart by exposing the reality of UFOs."

"I take your point, but I think the long-term effects of keeping the reality of UFOs and aliens a secret are worse than coming clean with the truth. Most of those think-tank studies were done during the Cold War by people with Cold War mentalities. People and attitudes have changed a lot since then. Our society has become more open and accepting of things that had once been taboo. Two good examples are marijuana and gay marriage. Another thing to consider is that to maintain the lie means hurting people. UFOs are a reality. People see them every day. Should we continue to make them look like fools? Should we continue to destroy the careers of professors who dare to take extraterrestrials seriously and study them? Should we continue killing abductees like my friend's ten-year-old daughter in what seems to be a futile effort to learn what the aliens are up to? I would argue that the minute The Seven is exposed and no longer poses a threat, we should tell the public what we know. Release every document, study, and photograph. I don't think our social order will fall apart. Maybe it would strengthen it. That seemed to be what Reagan hinted at in his U.N. speech when he mentioned aliens."

The President rattled the ice around in his crystal drink glass.

"I'm somewhat inclined to agree with you, Bill. But I wonder about doing everything at once. Do we crush The Seven and announce the reality of UFOs at the same time? Or do we take care of The Seven and then deal with the UFO question later and, perhaps, in piecemeal fashion? What do the rest of you think? Jake?"

"I agree with Bill, Sir. It's been secret too long. Get it out there."

"Ben?"

"Sir, I think I'm in the minority, but I believe we should maintain secrecy. I don't think our society and the world are ready for this reality."

"Max?"

"I also agree with Bill. We can't keep a secret like this much longer. Better to get it out."

"Cole?"

"When I brought you those photographs last year from NASA is when I became aware of the reality of the extraterrestrials, whoever they are and wherever they're from. At that time, I would have agreed with Ben. But after hearing Bill's account of his trip to Indiana and all that followed, I've changed my mind. But maybe for a slightly different reason. The aliens are totally in control. They do what they please and ignore us, unless they think we are threatening them. There is apparently nothing we can do about them or to them. Maybe at some point, they'll contact us and make their intentions known. I hope they are peaceful. But the government continuing to tell people what they are seeing with their own eyes is not real? That just doesn't strike me as a winning strategy anymore. What if we decide to continue on that path and shortly afterward the aliens decide to make contact with us? We would be exposed as a bunch of liars. The UFOs are here. Let's tell the truth and deal with it."

The President took a sip of his drink.

"Well, I've got a major decision to make, and I have to make it soon. Thanks for your views. Ben, you are in the minority. But, believe me, I appreciate your honesty and your willingness to take a contrary view. Now, if no one has any other pressing issues, I recommend we go inside and have dinner."

CHAPTER 18

Bill, Jake, and Cole lifted off from Joint Base Andrews at seven Wednesday morning in an Air Force Gulfstream G650 executive jet.

As soon as they reached cruising altitude, Bill and Jake filled Cole in on the plan to have Morgen pass a fake flash drive to Jake, who would then create a diversion. In the confusion, Morgen would then give the real drive to Bill, who would in turn give it to Cole so its contents could be forwarded to the President in the White House Situation Room.

Cole agreed it was a good idea in case one of the SEALs was compromised.

"What's your diversion, Jake?"

"It's still a work in progress."

"I'll bet."

✳

From the minute that the three stepped off the Gulfstream at Holloman, it was clear that Cole was in charge. The commanding general met them and assured Cole that the base was at his disposal. The four Black Hawks were lined up on the tarmac. Twenty-four Navy SEALs were gathered in a hanger, where Cole introduced himself to each one and also introduced Bill and Jake.

He then spoke to them as a group.

"Gentlemen, as I think you may know, we are going on a mission tonight under the direct orders and supervision of President Stanton. I am not at liberty to divulge details of the mission at this point except that it involves a possible incursion of Middle East terrorists across our border with Mexico. At twenty-two thirty a pilotless F-16 with ordinance aboard will be crashed on a large ranch near the border. Most of you and three of the Black Hawks will arrive within twenty minutes on what will appear to be a routine search and rescue mission. You will secure the crash site and the ranch house. Some civilians who live in the ranch house will probably have come outside after the crash. Direct them toward the barn and keep them away from the crash site. The fourth chopper will lag fifteen minutes behind as a backup. There will be six of you on each chopper. Bill Sanders and Jake McCoy will accompany me in the first chopper. The fact that the F-16 will not be manned is highly classified. You may get new orders after we arrive at the crash site. That's all I can tell you right now, and everything I've said is highly classified. Is that clear?

"Yes, Sir!" the SEALs replied in unison.

Bill and Jake spent the next hour getting outfitted with flight gear and helmets. They and Cole were offered quarters where they would be able to relax or sleep until the mission got under way.

As they were finishing with the flight gear, a sergeant driving a jeep pulled up to the hanger.

He saluted Cole and introduced himself as Sergeant Jones.

"Sir, there is a civilian at the main gate asking for a Jake McCoy. He says he's with you."

"He is. Hold on."

Cole motioned for Jake.

"Sergeant Jones says there a civilian at the front gate who wants to see you. Do you know anything about that?"

"Oh, yeah. Sergeant, can you give me a ride to the gate?"

"Yes, Sir. Hop in, Sir."

When Jake and Sergeant Jones returned, Jake was carrying a plastic picnic cooler, the kind that would just hold a six-pack of beer or soda, wrapped in military green duct tape. Cole and Bill give him puzzled looks but said nothing.

After dinner in the officers' mess, Cole, Bill, and Jake

rested in their assigned quarters as a dark, moonless night spread across the New Mexico desert.

✳

The starred sky was cloudless, and flames from the crashed F-16 were visible from several miles out as the three Black Hawks, flying at two thousand feet, approached the ranch.

Bill clung to his seat as the first helicopter touched down near the ranch's helipad with a sickening rocking motion. The other two helicopters landed nearby. Almost at once, eighteen heavily armed SEALs were on the ground and fanning out toward the ranch house and the crash site.

Bill, Jake, and Cole were the last ones out of their Black Hawk. Jake was carrying his duct-taped cooler.

Bill pulled the other two aside.

"Did you notice that SEAL sitting right across from me? The one with the scar on his cheek, just below his right eye."

Cole frowned.

"I did. What about him?"

"I didn't get good vibes from him. Nothing I can put my finger on. Just a feeling."

Jake looked at Cole.

"I agree with Bill. I think we need to keep an eye on him."

"Okay. But don't say or do anything without clearing it with me first."

Outdoor lights on the ranch house and barn were turned on, making visibility much better than Bill had expected. He looked toward the ranch house, where people were milling around and looking very confused. Right away, he spotted Morgen. Behind her was the tall bald man she had flown to New Mexico with. On her right was a boyish looking young man that Bill guessed was Jesse Copeland, the computer whiz who had given the file to Morgen.

Four of the SEALs started escorting the civilians toward the barn and corral. Cole, Bill, and Jake took a few steps forward, putting themselves directly in the path of the four SEALs and the group. Bill noticed that one of the SEALs was the man with the facial scar. In a whisper, he pointed that out to Cole and Jake. Both nodded.

As Bill looked back on what happened next, he would always remember it occurring in slow motion. In fact, it took less than a minute.

As the two groups merged, Morgen brushed against Jake. Out of the corner of his eye, Bill saw her slip a flash drive into his hand. Jake suddenly leaned over and placed the cooler he had been carrying on the ground. He tilted it on its side, pulled some tape from around the lid, and opened it. Out rolled a six-foot Western Diamondback rattlesnake, coiling and hissing and striking in every direction.

"Jesus Christ get back!" someone yelled. "It's a fucking rattlesnake."

Everyone moved back in unison, except Jake who was still bending over the cooler, which Bill only then noticed had several air holes drilled in the bottom. Morgen then slipped the second flash drive into Bill's hand and squeezed it tightly before backing away. By now, the snake had disappeared into the deep shadows around the barn.

Jake started to stand up when the SEAL with the scar pulled a combat knife from a leg sheath and attacked him. Both men went down. The SEAL was trying to pry the flash drive from Jake's right hand.

At that point, in Bill's memory, the slow motion stopped.

The normally calm and controlled Cole Favate took one step toward the struggling men and landed a bone-crunching kick into the right rib cage of the SEAL. Then Cole pulled him off Jake with a left-handed choke hold. The SEAL winched in pain but held onto his knife. With his right hand, Cole pulled a nine-millimeter Glock from its holster on his waist. He put the end of the barrel against the SEAL's head, just behind his right ear.

"Drop that knife, or I'll blow your fucking brains out through your eye sockets! Do it! NOW!"

The knife fell to the hard desert floor. Only then did Bill

notice that it was covered with blood.

Jake raised himself on one elbow.

"The fucker stabbed me in the thigh. I think it's bad."

Cole started barking orders to the other SEALs.

"Get a tourniquet around Jake's leg and get him aboard that chopper! Contact Holloman to have a medical team standing by. Bill and I will fly with him."

He pushed the SEAL he had been holding in a choke hold toward two others standing nearby.

"Arrest this son of a bitch and fly him back to Holloman after we leave. Lock him up in solitary until you get further orders from me. Is that clear?"

"Yes, Sir," both men said as they took custody of the SEAL.

Jake leaned close to Bill and whispered.

"You have it?"

"Yes."

Cole picked up the bloody knife as two other SEALs lifted Jake into the helicopter. Jake's left pants leg was soaked with blood, which dripped onto the ground and the helicopter. The tourniquet did not seem to be helping much.

Cole ordered the commander of the SEAL unit to continue to secure the ranch and remain there until further notice.

As the Black Hawk lifted off into the night, Bill caught a fleeting glimpse of Morgen standing near the corral.

By the time they were at flying altitude, Jake had grown pale and was moaning softly.

Cole shook his head.

"I'm afraid his femoral artery is severed."

Bill cradled Jake in his arms. Five minutes later he was dead.

It was after midnight when the Black Hawk touched down at Holloman, where it was met by a doctor and two nurses with a gurney. An ambulance was nearby, motor running.

Cole shook his head as the doctor approached the open

door of the helicopter.

"It's too late. He's dead. Let's get him on the gurney. Then get him into a body bag. We're flying him back to D.C. with us tonight."

After Jake's body was lifted onto the gurney and covered with a sheet, the doctor and nurses pushed the gurney toward the ambulance while Bill and Cole walked toward the head-quarters building next to the hanger.

They were met by Sergeant Jones, who saluted.

Cole returned the salute.

"Wake up the Gulfstream pilot and co-pilot, Sergeant Jones. Tell them we're flying back to Washington tonight, as soon as possible."

"Yes, Sir."

"But first, where is that secure computer I ordered?"

"This way, Sir."

When Bill and Cole were alone in a small office with the computer, Cole pulled out his iPhone and punched number seven. He turned on the speakerphone.

"Cole, talk to me."

"Mr. President, I'm on speakerphone with Bill Sanders. We have the flash drive containing the file. Within five min-utes, you should have it on your computer in the Situation Room."

"I'm on my way down there now."

"One more thing, Sir. I have some bad news."

"What?"

"Jake McCoy is dead. He was killed by one of the SEALs who was part of The Seven. I'll fill you in on the details later. I'm holding the SEAL in solitary at Holloman."

"Goddamn, I'm sorry to hear that. I liked that guy. Does he have any family I should call?"

Cole looked questioningly at Bill.

"No family," Bill said. "He was an only child. Divorced. No children. He had an on-again, off-again girlfriend. But I never met her and don't know her name."

"You heard that, Sir."

"Yes."

"Bill and I are flying back tonight with Jake's body. We'll make a printout of the file so we can read it on the plane."

"Good. I'll have a helicopter meet you at Andrews and bring you here. I'll also have an honor guard and a casket for Jake. Get back as fast as you can. If that file is what we think it is, I'll need Bill's writing talents."

"We'll move as fast as we can sir. See you later in the morning."

∗

When the eastbound Gulfstream hit cruising altitude, Cole made sure the door to the cockpit was closed. From a small case he had brought on the plane, he pulled two hard copies of the file that was on the flash drive. Each was twenty pages. He handed one to Bill and started to read the other.

Neither of them said a word as they read.

Cole finished first. Bill, five minutes later.

Bill spoke first.

"Cole, this is like some fucking nightmare."

"Worse than that. It's real. And it's set to come down a week from today."

"I can't believe that The Seven went from a secret group trying to cover up UFOs to this. If I'm going to help Stanton write an address, I need to make some notes. Help me sort through this. Talk me through it."

Bill pulled a reporter's notebook out of his backpack.

Cole took a sip of water from a bottle.

"Well, this document makes it clear that Ross Duncan, the Senate majority leader, is the head of The Seven and Bob Walker, the CIA director, is number two. But, Jesus, look at the other five members. A Nobel-prize winning scientist, a federal appeals court judge, the CEO of a newspaper chain, a bird colonel working for the Joint Chiefs at the Pentagon, and the chairman of the House Ways and Means Committee. What the hell is wrong with these people?"

"Jake, they're only the tip of the iceberg. Remember all those other names on Warren Holden's lists, which we're sure was nowhere near reflective of the total."

"I know. I keep thinking of Jim Winston."

"Maybe some of them were being blackmailed or threatened in some way. Maybe they got caught up in something that got out of hand. Maybe they're just evil, destructive people. Maybe they crave power, no matter what the costs."

"Well, they apparently think their dreams will come true next Thursday. Look at the second paragraph on page five. They'll try to lure Stanton to that so-called training exercise the CIA is staging in Maryland near Camp David. They plan to use some exotic nerve gas on him and his Secret Service detail to render them unconscious. Then they'll take Stanton hostage. They'll keep him alive as long as he's useful to them. They they'll kill him. At the same time that they capture Stanton, they'll unleash a number of assassinations at the Pentagon, on the Hill, at federal agencies, and in the West Wing. They'll also go after top governors around the country. Their agents are everywhere, including networks and major news organizations. And look at this. They have guns that can pass through metal detectors unnoticed."

Bill signaled for Cole to pause while he made some notes.

Cole turned to page 12 of the document.

"Jake predicted this. At the same time the President is being kidnapped and a wave of assassinations is sweeping the nation, there will be a dozen precisely coordinated 9/11-type attacks on high-profile targets, including the Supreme Court building, the Capitol, the Sears Tower in Chicago, The Golden Gate Bridge in San Francisco, the Space Needle in Seattle, the Empire State Building, the Bellagio in Las Vegas ...."

"They say they'll use small corporate jets. Can they pull that off?"

"They can the way they have it planned. They've got twelve small jets full of fuel and crammed with explosives parked at private airports near their targets. They've recruited and trained Middle East jihadist zealots to fly the plans into the targets. It says here that the families of the suicide pilots will be paid ten million dollars each by The Seven."

"That fits with what they did when they blew up the airliner my wife was on."

"As soon as the President is seized and the assassinations have begun, the planes will take off and head for their targets. They'll have it timed to hit all the targets at once. The Air Force wouldn't have a chance of stopping them. In the following confusion, Duncan and Walker will seize power, probably vowing to bring the evildoers to justice."

"What about the Vice-President?"

"I guess they're counting on him and the Speaker of the House being dead by then. Or at least incapacitated."

"This is insane. Even if they fail, they will have done monumental damage to the country."

"Which is why we have to stop them."

As the Gulfstream sped toward the dawn sky, Cole dozed off while Bill started outlining a draft speech for the President.

CHAPTER 19

The President pressed the button beneath the edge of his desk that shut off audio and video recordings of the Oval Office, making it "dark." It was almost noon. Gathered around the Resolute Desk were Ben Watkins, Cole Favate, Max Burris, and Bill Sanders.

The President looked up from a briefing paper he was reading.

"That's awful news about Jake. Unfortunately, we'll have to grieve later. And we will. But right now, we have to move fast. Jake would have wanted that. Max, call the networks and tell them I want airtime at four for a major address to the nation. I just talked to the Secretary of State and we're notifying every nation with which we have diplomatic relations that this speech is highly important and involves them."

"Wouldn't it be better to give the speech at night? The audience would be bigger."

"But it would seem too ordinary. I want this to be perceived as the emergency it is. Interrupt some soap operas. Plus, we need daylight. Go, Max. Do it now. We need time to set up TV cameras in here."

"Yes, Sir. On my way."

The President turned to Bill.

"I was just reading the draft of the speech you wrote. It's good, but too general. It lacks the specifics of the actions I plan to take, which you had no way of knowing. Here's a list of the things I plan to do. Can you work them into your version and have it ready for me to review by three? That'll give us a few minutes to make last-minutes changes."

"Yes, Sir. I can do that. You're okay with my take on how to handle E.T.?"

"Couldn't you guess from my comments earlier? Look, I've got work to do. Let's meet back here at three. Ben, is everything under control in your department?"

"It is, Sir. I've increased security around the White House."

"Good. Cole, I need you to stay here with me. I've asked Mark Smith, one of the White House lawyers to join us. He's an expert on the Constitution and presidential power in the wake of 9/11."

"We're going outside our group?"

"At this point it doesn't matter. I've briefed the Vice President and the Chief of Staff. They were pissed to be left out of the loop, but they understood. They'll get over it."

✳

Bill, Max, Cole, and Mark Smith were standing behind the camera as the President adjusted his tie, took a sip of water, and handed the glass to a steward.

Thirty seconds later, President Samuel Stanton looked directly into the camera and a teleprompter and began to speak in his deep and authoritative voice.

My fellow Americans and fellow citizens of the world. I am speaking to you this afternoon because this country faces an attempted coup from a powerful, secret group that has been operating within our government since the end of the Second World War.

The group is called The Seven. It was created by President Truman to contain and control the growing phenomenon of unidentified flying objects, or UFOs, and the aliens that control them. Truman and a handful of aides knew it was impossible to keep UFOs a secret in a democracy with a free press. The seven members of the group were given the authority to select their own successors independent of the White House or any other parts of the government. They operate with black budgets hidden deep within other black budgets of the CIA and the National Security Agency, as well as their counterparts in other major industrialized nations. Until now, only two presidents since Tru-

man—John F. Kennedy and Ronald Reagan—knew of The Seven's existence and mission. Over the years, The Seven has manipulated public opinion to make UFOs and those who report seeing them seem ridiculous, while at the same time creating a narrative that the government has some secret agreement with the aliens and knowledge of what's going on. But what The Seven has really been covering up is that the government knows nothing about UFOs or aliens. They ignore us and efforts to contact them have been futile. More about that in a few minutes.

The Seven's original mission made some sense at the beginning of the Cold War and with it the growing threat of nuclear weapons. Studies from prestigious think tanks all warned of dire consequences if the government were to acknowledge the reality of life elsewhere more advanced than ours.

Over the decades, The Seven has grown powerful and strayed far from its original goal, the inevitable fate of secret organizations with too much power and too much money. It has secretly enlisted thousands of ordinary citizens and officials into its ranks, sometimes through blackmail and threats and even murder. It has become a danger to the social and political order far greater than any secret it was trying to cover up. The Seven has become what it was created to prevent: a broken, lawless society.

We learned of The Seven and its plot to overthrow the government because an American writer name Bill Sanders traveled to Indiana last year to help an old friend find his missing ten-year-old daughter. The friend claimed she was abducted by a UFO. That was true. She was later kidnapped and killed by The Seven as part of an effort to uncover the aliens' purpose. Mr. Sanders discovered a set of lists of numerous government and elected officials involved with The Seven. He also discovered some secret photographs from NASA that clearly showed UFOs, both on the moon and Mars. Oddly enough, at around the same time I was given similar photos from a NASA source. Those lists and photos are being released to the press as I speak. It was only when Mr. Sanders and I crossed paths via my press secretary, Max Burris, that the pieces of the puzzle began to fall into place. We had to meet and operate in a very tight secret group because of our uncertainty about The Seven's reach. My previous press secretary, Jim Winston, who recently committed suicide, was also involved with The Seven, as were three Secret Service agents assigned to the White House.

It was then that we learned of Operation Snakebite, The Seven's plan for a coup. Last night, in a classified military operation in New Mexico, we were able to secure a copy of The Seven's written plans for Snakebite, a detailed and incriminating document called The New Order. The twenty-page document also gave more information about The Seven's top leaders. Copies are also being released to the press as I speak. The Seven's CEO, for lack of a better term, is Ross Duncan, the majority leader of the United States Senate. His second in command is Robert Walker, the director of the CIA, who was my roommate in college and, I thought, a friend.

According to the document, Operation Snakebite involved three simultaneous operations next Thursday.

First, I was invited by Walker to attend a CIA training session in Maryland near Camp David. I had agreed to go. Once there, my Secret Service detail and I were to be incapacitated by a nerve gas. I would then be held hostage in case I was needed. When I was no longer needed, I was to be killed.

Second, at the time I was to be captured, The Seven planned to unleash a series of assassinations at the Pentagon, on the Hill, at federal agencies, and in the West Wing. Their targets presumably were to include the Vice President and the Speaker of the House. They were also planning to kill top governors around the country, as well as seize control of the networks and major news organizations. Their agents would be stationed near their targets and ready to move as soon as they got the word that I had been seized. They would use guns that can pass through metal detectors unnoticed.

Third, while I was being held captive and a wave of assassinations was sweeping the nation, there were to be a dozen precisely coordinated 9/11-type attacks on high-profile targets, including the Supreme Court building, the Capitol, the Empire State Building, and The Golden Gate Bridge. These attacks were to use small corporate jets full of fuel and crammed with explosives that are presently parked at private airports near their targets. The attacks were to be coordinated to hit all the targets at the same time. The Seven recruited and trained Middle East jihadist zealots to fly the planes into the targets. The families of the twelve suicide pilots were to be paid ten million dollars each by The Seven.

Amid the chaos expected from these three simultaneous acts of terror, Ross Duncan and Robert Walker planned to seize power, and with the help of The Seven's network of secret agents and members, take over the government. They would promise to restore calm and order to the terror and disorder they had caused.

None of this will happen because, under powers granted me by the United States Constitution and emergency legislation passed by the Congress following 9/11, I am taking the following action:

First, I am immediately imposing martial law in all fifty states. I am also federalizing the National Guard in the states.

Second, I am invoking the Insurrection Act, which will allow United States military personnel to aid the National Guard and federal law enforcement officials.

Both these moves will be temporary and will be lifted as soon as the threat The Seven poses is fully under control. That should be in a matter of days or a few weeks, at most.

As I speak to you this afternoon, FBI agents, with help from the Secret Service and the military, have arrested Ross Duncan and Bob Walker and the other five top members of The Seven. They will be jailed without bail and charged with treason. The scores of government and elected officials on the lists I mention earlier will also be tracked down, arrested, and charged with treason.

We know that the top members of The Seven and those on the lists are only the tip of the iceberg. We will use every tool at our disposal to track down and arrest as many people as we can find who are involved with The Seven.

The Seven maintained two main bases of operation complete with underground bunkers and sophisticated electronics and communications equipment. One is on a ten-thousand-acre ranch is southern New Mexico near the border. This is where we were able to acquire a copy of The New Order. The other base in on an Ulster County farm in New York state, less than a hundred miles north of New York City. Navy SEALs have secured the New Mexico ranch and are in the process of raiding and securing the Ulster County operation.

In addition, United States military and national guard troops are seizing control of the twelve airports from which the 9/11-type attacks were to be launched. The jets will be impounded and disarmed of their explosives.

Let me assure you that this will not turn into a witch hunt. We know, for instance, that a number of lower-level employees of The Seven probably had no idea what was going on. They will not be arrested or charged without compelling evidence. We are not imposing any lockdowns or curfews unless circumstances change.

Now let me turn to the subjects of unidentified flying objects and aliens. I have spoken of them as though they are a reality. That's because they are. We think they have been a reality on Earth for thousands, if not hundreds of thousands of years.

For decades now, our government and other governments of the world have gone to great lengths to cover up the existence of UFOs. But as we know from The Seven, what we have covered up is not what we know but what we don't know.

It is time to tell the truth. It is time to stop making people who have seen a UFO or had an experience of some kind with them appear ridiculous. While not every strange light in the sky is a UFO, we must make room for the ones that are.

The hard truth is that we know nothing about UFOs and the aliens who operate them. Efforts to contact them have been fruitless. They ignore us except when they think we are threatening them. Along with the photos of UFOs on the moon and Mars, I am also releasing portions of a letter written to Bill Sanders by the late Colonel Richard West, who was a top operative for The Seven. The letter was delivered to Mr. Sanders six months after West's death. The letter will explain what has been going on in much more detail than I can go into in a single speech.

The aliens—there appear be more than one type of them—appear to be benign. Are they cooperating with each other or here on separate agendas? We don't know. While some abductees have reported negative experiences, the vast majority are either neutral or positive.

But to repeat: We don't know. We don't know where the aliens are from or why they are interested in us. Are they from another planet in our vast universe? Are they from another dimension, as some have speculated? Are they the human race from the future when time travel has become possible, as others propose? Why are they so interested in us? Are they monitoring our evolutionary development? Are they interfering with it? Are they responsible for cattle mutilations and crop circles?

Again, let me emphasize: We do not know.

Among the reasons for the coverup is that governments do not like to admit they are not in control. Especially when UFOs have been sighted around military and nuclear installations. Studies by NASA and Brookings and RAND have recommended secrecy because of the fear of social and political disruptions that would occur otherwise. The studies feared religious and economic convulsions. The breakdown of our civil society. Rioting. A stock market debacle.

I profoundly disagree. These studies were done during the Cold War and reflected the fears of the time. I think we have moved on. I think the American people and the people of other nations can handle the truth. Recent polls show a majority think UFOs are real. It is unreasonable for the government to continue to cover up what thousands of Americans, including police and members of the military, see every year with their own eyes and pick up on radar. The government, I believe, is only fooling itself.

Therefore, I am ordering the declassification and release of all UFO-related documents held by any government agency, including the CIA, the military, the FBI, and the NSA. This cannot be done overnight. It may take months. But it will be done. The only exceptions I will allow—and those exceptions must be approved by me on a case-by-case basis—are if the release of a document would endanger someone, like a secret agent or an informant.

I do not know where this action will lead. I don't know if the aliens will notice or care. What I do know is that in a democracy, we should err on the side of truth and openness. We will get through the threat posed by The Seven. Then our real adventure begins. We are not alone. Let us make the most of it. If the aliens are listening, we welcome them and offer our friendship and cooperation.

God bless America and all the people of the Earth. Thank you. Good luck and Godspeed.

CHAPTER 20

Southwest Harbor, Maine: A Year Later

Bill Sanders and Morgen Remley had just finished having lunch on the deck of a small oceanfront house Bill had bought a year ago as a getaway from the New York media circus.

Bill's cell phone rang. He glanced at it. It was Nancy Luke. "Hello, Nancy."

"Bill, are you and Morgen okay? I haven't heard from you since we delivered the manuscript to the publisher."

"We're good. Just relaxing and bracing for the media shitstorm when the book comes out in the fall. By the way, are they happy with my title?

"Absolutely. *Starfall* it will be. With a subtitle: *The Seven and the Reality of UFOs.*"

"Well, if somebody comes up with something better, I'm open to changing it."

"I'll pass that along, but I think it works. They think so, too."

"At least now I can get back to work on *Power Points.*"

"Yes, but when *Starfall* is published, you're going to be busy for many weeks with interviews and tours. You were sure right about the publisher being willing to postpone *Power Points.* But that's because we offered them *Starfall* without a bidding war. If we had opened it up for bids, we could have gotten a bigger advance, but we probably would have had to fight a lawsuit over delaying *Power Points.* And the advance we got is not exactly small. You know I would never have initially resisted this if I had known the truth."

"I know, Nancy. But you understand why I couldn't tell you everything until it was over."

"Yes, of course I do. You were also right to refuse any interviews or comments following the President's speech and the announcement that you were writing *Starfall*. I thought you were blowing a big opportunity for free publicity for the book. But by your remaining silent, the demand for the book has become overwhelming. Everybody wants to hear your story. It's going to sell millions and millions of copies. It could turn out to be one of the top best-selling books ever."

"Let's hope so."

"And don't forget that the movie version of *Look Down* will be coming out just before Christmas. Word is that Brett Cooper is likely to be nominated for an Academy Award for best actor and the film for best picture."

"I'm sorry I wasn't able to get back to Jefferson for the actual filming."

"Well, that not exactly a place of happy memories for you. By the way, have you heard or seen any indications that the aliens are aware that we've acknowledged their reality? It's been a year."

"Nope, not a thing. Maybe they don't read papers or listen to the news. Maybe their concept of time isn't the same as ours. Maybe our year is a minute or a day to them. Who knows? We may never know any more than we know now, which is basically nothing. And if they did make contact, I wouldn't be among the first to know. I've never even seen a UFO, except in my dreams. Well, I guess there were those childhood episodes that Paul Watson wrote about that involved me. But I have no memory of them."

"I was just reading a long essay in the Atlantic by a Harvard professor I've never hear of and whose name I can't remember about the reactions in the weeks and months following the President's speech. It seems Stanton was right. There was no social, economic, or political disruptions. In fact, this professor argues, everyone seems to have relaxed a bit. People aren't as divisive as they had been. National and international tensions have eased. It seems that the fact we are not alone has been reassuring in an odd way. Like we're trying to show our good side to guests."

"I think there's some truth to that. I touch on it a bit at the end of *Starfall*."

"I know. I'll mail the article to you. By the way, we haven't had one of our lunches in a long time. I miss them."

"I do, too. We'll pick up again when I come back to New York early in the fall."

"Take care. I'll be in touch if anything comes up."

"Thanks, Nancy."

Morgen poured more wine into both their glasses.

"What are you going to do with the car?" She gestured toward the red 1963 Studebaker Avanti parked below the deck.

"I don't know for sure. Keep it, I guess. Jake left it to me in a handwritten codicil to his will, along with twenty thousand dollars for what he described as its 'care and feeding.' How can I do anything but keep it? It also carries some memories for me because it's the car Jake and I used when we drove around the West mailing those lists and photos to members of The Seven. Jake knew I didn't have much interest in or knowledge about cars, but I don't think he knew anyone else who would appreciate it. So, I guess we'll drive it back to New York in a few weeks and park it in my building. We can use it to get out of town now and then. It is fun to drive, even though it often draws more attention than I like."

"Bill, the secretive loner."

"I'm getting better about that, you must admit."

"Yes, you are. What about us?"

"What about us?"

"We've been together for a year now and make a pretty good match. We love each other. What comes next?"

"More of the same? Do you want to get married?"

"Not necessarily."

"I agree. I don't see much point in it. I've rewritten my will to take care of you, so that's not an issue. When the *Starfall* publicity circus dies down, and before I get back to work on *Power Points*, I suggest we take a long vacation to some exotic place, maybe the South Pacific."

Morgen leaned over and kissed Bill.

"Good idea."

A cloud passed over the sun, throwing the balcony into shadow. Morgen frowned.

"Tell me something, Bill. What's your most powerful memory of the past couple of years?"

"No question about that. It was when Stanton told me that the SEALs at the New Mexico ranch had you in a helicopter on the way to Holloman and D.C."

The sun peeked from behind the cloud.

"I have one other question. Where do you think the fact that UFOs and aliens have been acknowledged as a reality will lead us?"

"Who knows? It's not up to us, is it?"

— THE END —

ABOUT THE AUTHOR

Fred Ellis Brock is the author of the best-selling *Retire on Less Than You Think: The New York Times Guide to Planning Your Financial Future* (2nd Edition – Times Books/Henry Holt, 2008); *Health Care on Less Than You Think: The New York Times Guide to Getting Affordable Coverage* (Times Books/Henry Holt, 2006); and *Live Well on Less Than You Think: The New York Times Guide to Achieving Your Financial Freedom* (Times Books/Henry Holt, 2005). For more than a decade he was a business editor and columnist at The New York Times. For six years he wrote that paper's "Seniority" column and was the author of the "Off the Rack" media column prior to that. He has also worked as an editor and reporter for The Wall Street Journal, The Houston Chronicle and The Louisville Courier-Journal. He holds an M.Ed. from Temple University and a B.A. in English literature from Hanover College. He has taught undergraduate and graduate reporting and editing at New York University and Kansas State University, where he held the R.M. Seaton Professional Journalism Chair. He was a fellow at the Washington Journalism Center, with a concentration in public affairs reporting. He lives in Arizona, where he teaches at the University of Arizona and is a contributor to The New York Times and a featured speaker for the Times Journeys travel program. He is represented by the David Black Literary Agency and AEI Speakers Bureau.

Brock, while pursuing conventional journalism and teaching careers, has been interested in UFO sightings and science fiction since he was in high school. He is a member of the Mutual UFO Network (MUFON) and has witnessed unexplained sightings in the U.S. and Europe. He has interviewed scores of witnesses to UFO sightings for both articles and personal research; he has read widely on the subject. All this is reflected in the authenticity of *The Seven*.

CPSIA information can be obtained
at www.ICGtesting.com
Printed in the USA
BVHW081938130421
604813BV00005B/422